Columbia in Manhattanville

Edited by Caitlin Blanchfield
Columbia Books on Architecture and the City

Schools of architecture often focus their attentions outward, exploring the broadest array of sites and concerns that design might touch on. But another role of a school of architecture is to look thoughtfully at its own university, not simply as the context within which we teach and learn but as an architectural project. Columbia University—in its existing campus, its extensive real estate holdings, and particularly its soon-to-open expansion between 125th Street and 133rd Street on Manhattan's West Side, a neighborhood historically known as Manhattanville—is one such ongoing architectural project, effecting lasting changes (spatially, economically, politically, culturally) on the city around it.

The design and construction of Manhattanville will be seen as one of the principal legacies of Lee C. Bollinger's tenure as Columbia University's president. Planning began in 2003, shortly after his appointment, with the plan earning final approval in 2009 and construction beginning not long after. It is a complex story—a university bursting at the seams, the changing imperatives of research facilities, large-scale investment in underground infrastructures, a controversial use of eminent domain, the commissioning of celebrated architects, and a remarkable campaign of community engagement all combining to reshape the public face of a venerable institution.

This book began with the invitation of Renzo Piano—the designer, with Skidmore, Owings & Merrill, of the Manhattanville master plan and the architect of the campus's first two buildings—to speak at Columbia University's Graduate School of Architecture, Planning, and Preservation in March 2015. It then expanded into a larger research and publication project, led by editor Caitlin Blanchfield and assisted at various moments by Alissa Anderson, James Folta, Robin Hartanto Honggare, Isabelle Kirkham-Lewitt, and Gabrielle Printz. The resulting volume opens up several different ways of thinking about Columbia's interventions in Manhattanville—a kind of architectural self-examination. It assembles interviews with many of the key players in the project's creation, as well as its future inhabitants; it asks us to attend to the longer history of repeated attempts at new plans for Manhattanville, and Columbia's role within the social fabric of Harlem; it collects a series of essays that consider the campus in situ but also as an indication of broader tendencies within the development of the contemporary university; and finally, it visually documents a slice of time in its construction, showing that master plans have as much to do with directing change as with reaching end states.

It will be many years yet before the new Manhattanville campus is fully built out; this book is being published just as its first buildings are being occupied. What follows is a reflection on a moment of transition from within that moment, marking something of a midpoint in a conversation about the university and the city that began with the project's origins in 2003 and that will continue well into the future.

James Graham
Director of Publications
Columbia University GSAPP

Table of Contents

Preface
Lee C. Bollinger

In 2003, when I proposed in my inaugural address that space was a critical element in the future of Columbia University and that I believed Columbia's future should be within our home community of West Harlem, I knew several things: I knew that Columbia's intellectual ambitions could not be achieved without major new physical space. I knew that, ever since competing visions of urban planning collided in the heated controversy over Columbia's proposed Morningside Park gym in the late 1960s, Columbia's capacity to fulfill the ever-increasing potential of a great American research university had been physically limited. I knew that a piecemeal, building-by-building approach to growth in our community would take too long and probably ultimately fail; and that a larger vision—a smart urban plan for an entire new campus—held the greater likelihood of success.

I knew that Columbia had to embrace Harlem and upper Manhattan as its home and neighbors, with all the longtime challenges and special magic that coexist in this iconic community. I knew that the building of a new campus in the industrial area known as Manhattanville had to be seized as a moment to project the intellectual excitement of new knowledge, including the remarkable creativity in art and culture that we are encountering in this new century. And I knew that the physical buildings and spaces had to be approached with the same expectation of creativity that we would bring to the academic work taking place in that new campus. At the same time, I believed strongly that we had to create a new and different kind of academic space that would both serve our own mission and be a welcome addition to our city. What I didn't know was how daunting the challenge of achieving this vision would be. Fortunately, countless numbers of supremely talented people (many mentioned in or part of this volume), within the university and outside, including our elected and appointed officials, dedicated a good portion of their lives to bringing these ideas and values to reality.

Columbia's Graduate School of Architecture, Planning, and Preservation has been a vital partner in the Manhattanville project. Mark Wigley and now Amale Andraos, as deans, have been friends, colleagues, and advisors in the long process. The school has played many roles, most notably as a kind of conscience reminding us of the need to keep physical planning and design in close alignment with the intellectual and human ambitions inherent in something of this scale. Now it is time for self-reflection, and there is no better way to do that than through a work like this book. I am, therefore, extremely grateful for and admiring of the school, and Amale, for undertaking this project. We are only at the beginning of the journey, and this book will play a significant role in shaping how we should look ahead.

The Manhattanville Grid
Amale Andraos

The grid has served as an urbanizing and colonizing device since ancient times. The Romans deployed it around the Mediterranean basin to construct their empire of networked towns, cities, and military outposts. From Timgad (100 AD) to Lancaster (80 AD), the perfectly centuriated landscape organized around the coupled axes of the *decumanus maximus* and the *cardo maximus* embedded Roman knowledge, power, and infrastructure equally into widely diverse landscapes and cultures. The Spanish conquistadores embraced the Roman model of the grid as an effective tool for settling "New World" cities such as Santo Domingo (1650). The grid

1834 map of Chicago, based on the Land Ordinance of 1785 drafted by Thomas Jefferson, a schema that required land in western territories be laid out in square parcels.

could also evenly negotiate between the urban, the rural, and the natural: a committed agrarian, Thomas Jefferson extolled his checkerboard grid for its power to tame the "pestilences" and "miasmas" of the city and find equilibrium between density and open green space. This same delicate balance also preoccupied Le Corbusier's regulating and gridded Radiant City.[1]

The grid did not just mediate difference in the landscape, it was used to segregate as well: in the sixteenth and seventeenth centuries, the grid was used to isolate infected bodies to control the spread of the plague in French towns.[2] In the early nineteenth century, the grid demarcated the "wild" from the "civilized" as the orthogonal planning of Manhattan flattened the Lenape tribe's "Island of Many Hills" into equally developable plots of land. Even as an anti-urban device, such as with Frank Lloyd Wright's Broadacre City, the grid was deployed to domesticate the natural into a series of equally manageable agricultural plots.

This familiar reading of the grid exists alongside another reading that, in contrast, has long embraced the grid for the seemingly *opposite*

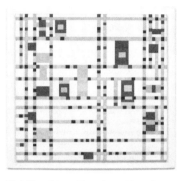

Piet Mondrian, *Broadway Boogie Woogie*, 1942–1943. Copyright of the Museum of Modern Art/Licensed by SCALA/Art Resource, NY.

effects and possibilities it produces: the infinite freedom of an abstracted, universal, and generic field that can undo the frames it constructs, suggesting endless expansion and implying a form of organization within which maximum individual difference and specificity are not only possible but also desirable. This notion of the grid animated the early modernist experiments of artists and architects alike, from Russian Constructivism to De Stijl and the Bauhaus. Their plastic experiments ushered in new relationships between the universal and the specific, opening up an inspired and still productive conversation between part and whole, frame and framed, inside

1
WORKac, *49 Cities* (New York: Inventory Press, 2015).

2
Michel Foucault, *Security, Territory, Population: Lectures at the Collège de France 1977–1978*, trans. Graham Burchell (New York: Picador, 2009), 10.

3
Rem Koolhaas, *Delirious New York: A Retroactive Manifesto for Manhattan* (New York: Oxford University Press, 1978).

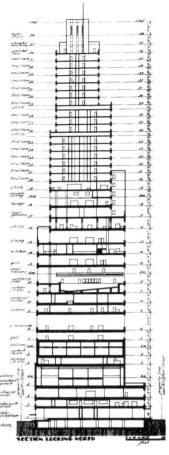

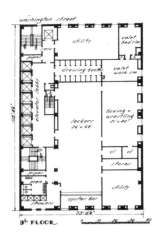

The thirty-nine floors of the Downtown Athletic Club, juxtaposing a range of programs in both section and plan. Published in Rem Koolhaas's *Delirious New York: A Retroactive Manifesto for Manhattan*.

and outside. Piet Mondrian's Boogie Woogie series is one of the best embodiments of this conversation. Not surprisingly, it was New York—the city's architecture, its urban form, and its jazz music—that inspired the Dutch painter's famously dynamic and lively gridded compositions. And it was *Delirious New York*,[3] Rem Koolhaas's seminal retroactive manifesto for the city that rehabilitated the grid during a moment of reckoning for the modernist project,[4] as he re-read the many potential freedoms it holds: the generic and universal field it creates, the individualized expression and formal extravagances it enables, the sectional and social encounters it produces, and the exceptional and even utopian moments it frames.[5] As a result of this avant-garde fascination, it is today no longer the grid that suggests settling, segregation, and control but rather, the "ladders,"

bucolic wiggly roads, and cul-de-sac patterns of suburban developments that have become the model for gated communities and defensible spaces.[6]

It could be said that these two readings of the grid demonstrate how form exists independently from its performance, as a particular generation of architects invested in the notion of "autonomy" has argued.[7] This position invites

architecture and urban form making to disengage from the sociopolitical, economic, and cultural context they exist in and shape—even as these resulting "autonomous" buildings have repeatedly contributed both positively and negatively to their context.[8] Columbia's Manhattanville campus expansion offers a unique outlook on this dialectic; unlike any other architectural and urban experiment of its kind today, Manhattanville collapses these two readings of the grid, as well as their very real consequences and future possibilities, as an equally compelling and charged urban and architectural proposition for our time. On the one hand is the expansion into and transformation of an existing community and its surrounding context, the opposed narratives of eminent domain and a complex process of community engagement.[9] On the other is the embrace of the freedom and openness enabled by the grid, both as the main organizing principle of the master plan and at the architectural scale—in plan, section, and elevation—of the first buildings inaugurating the campus, thus setting the context for buildings to come.[10]

Of course, the Manhattan grid already shaped Manhattanville. But the idea of embracing the grid in its modernist sense of accessibility, connection, and continuity, as a democratic form that can hold together individual freedom and difference, for a private university campus whose research and academic functions would be anything but open

4
Although postmodern in its "retroactive" narrative, *Delirious New York* stands in contrast to the flurry of other critiques of modernism like Aldo Rossi's *The Architecture of the City* (1984), Robert Venturi's *Complexity and Contradiction in Architecture* (1977), and Colin Rowe's *Collage City* (1984).

5
See Albert Pope, *Ladders* (New York: Princeton Architectural Press, 1996); and *Foreclosed: Rehousing the American Dream*, New York, Museum of Modern Art, February–August 2012, for recent critiques on suburban form and development.

6
Pope, *Ladders*.

7
For a compelling summary of Autonomy versus Engagement, see Peter Eisenman and Rem Koolhaas, *AA Words One: Supercritical* (London: AA Publications, 2007).

8
While Frank Gehry's Guggenheim Museum Bilbao revitalized the city's infrastructure and economy, Peter Eisenman's City of Culture complex in Galicia contributed to the region's economic collapse.

9
See Steven Gregory, "The Radiant University: Space, Urban Development, and the Public Good," in this volume, 110–125; and Maxine Griffith, "Manhattanville: A Personal History," in this volume, 96–107.

10
See Renzo Piano, "The University in the City: Renzo Piano in Conversation with Amale Andraos, and Nicolai Ouroussoff," in this volume, 16–27.

and accessible, is in itself a radical proposition. This is true not only for the immediate encounter between Columbia University and the surrounding Harlem community but, just as importantly, for the future of the university in general, as a site of knowledge at once removed from and embedded within the world. The construction of university campuses is flourishing all over the world, from Qatar to Abu Dhabi and from Weifang to Zhengzhou, and many of these new institutions default to the model of the bucolic and removed American campus—with its winding paths, green quadrants, beautiful building-objects, and gated boundaries, often turning this characteristic layout into branded "knowledge cities." At such a moment, it seems important to underscore the qualities of a project that declares, in its architectural and urban form, the future of the university as decidedly urban, with all the challenges and opportunities that a serious commitment to engaging the world produces.

But a grid in plan, as *Delirious New York* once proclaimed, is only as democratic as the life, architectural and

Renzo Piano Building Workshop and Richard Rogers, Centre Georges Pompidou, Paris, 1977. Photograph by Michel Denancé. Courtesy of Renzo Piano Building Workshop.

programmatic, it enables in section—the urban "culture of congestion" that produces unexpected encounters and possibilities, such as Koolhaas's famous example of "eating oysters with boxer gloves, naked, on the nth floor" of New York's Downtown Athletic Club.[11] Renzo Piano, an ardent modernist and master of the exquisite articulation, layering, and tectonic of the generic plane, knows that well. In keeping, his buildings are often an assembled whole of individually identifiable parts that remain open-ended. But the Italian architect's interests

have rarely focused on the layered section's capacity to work as a "social condenser" (a term Koolhaas borrowed from the Constructivists), and the formal and programmatic consequences that ensue. Rather, it is within the envelope that his architectural commitments have been most clear—as a space of endless movement and poetic negotiation of air, light, and people that inhabit and animate the various boundaries between inside and outside. Piano's mastery of the envelope was first evident in the Centre Georges Pompidou, where the interior circulation of people and air was "turned inside out" to become the museum's exterior façade—a strategy he embraced in part again for the new Whitney Museum's outdoor sequence of terraces and stairs. Similarly, the skilled thickening of ceiling cavities to light museum galleries—from his seminal Menil Collection building in Houston to the Nasher Museum in Dallas— have rendered his buildings unique calibrators of light.

In Manhattanville, Piano's first two buildings act in dialogue, as if forming an intensive exploration of building envelopes and their ability to articulate and complicate three-dimensionally the boundaries they are given as site. By staging his strongly opaque Lenfest Center for the Arts—a compact volume whose mass is turned light by

Renzo Piano Building Workshop, Whitney Museum, New York, 2016. Photograph by Nic Lehoux. Courtesy of Renzo Piano Building Workshop.

Renzo Piano Building Workshop, the Menil Collection, Houston, 1986. Photograph by Paul Hester. Courtesy of Piano & Fitzgerald, Fondazione Renzo Piano.

the jewel-like treatment of its articulated parts and exterior finishes—against the Jerome L. Greene Science Center, whose mammoth footprint is rendered almost ethereal by its astonishingly transparent skin, a transparency only a few architects have succeeded in achieving, Piano once again renders lightness as the driving concept of his architecture. This transparency is most striking from the elevated 1 train, as one's gaze penetrates into the depth of the building, seeing right through it. For Piano, architecture is not a conceptual practice but an experiential one. Buildings are not intended to become spectacle, but rather to become solid anchors in the urban fabric, as they carry the generic qualities of the modernist grid in plan into the details of their highly articulated elevations. For Manhattanville's first pair of buildings, Piano's almost utilitarian expression is both an appropriate and welcome resonance with the site's industrial past. On the ground, the classic modernist *piloti*—columns that raise the bulk of the building to allow passage beneath—is reinterpreted with glass planes and performed through a trimming of the layers above, as surfaces recede and become more transparent as they meet the ground, giving lightness to the mass above in a

kind of "lifting" that he loves.

But like the grid, the history of transparency in architecture is not so clear. On the one hand, there is the effect of openness, accessibility, and literal as well as phenomenal "transparency."[12] On the other, the use of transparent barriers for increasingly more private, inaccessible, defensive, and unknowable spaces. From the transformation of banks, which in the mid-1950s abandoned their classical fortress-like expression to become modernist "glass fish bowls" at the moment when financial markets and flows of money became increasingly *less* transparent,[13] to the contemporary hysteria with glass skins that now shield the most exclusive new residential buildings in the city, "transparency" today is well understood as a double-edged knife that can reveal and welcome or hide and keep at bay.[14] But just as the grid holds together conflicting intentions and possibilities, architecture

can never be reduced to form and material alone. Architecture is not only what it is; it is also what it does.[15] It is not *what* it represents but *how* it represents.[16] Architecture is a synthetic field, and buildings are the synthesis of many parts, not all of which are strictly "material." The social and cultural life of buildings—their use, programs, events, connections—as well as the economics and politics of their making and use, past and future, all contribute to whether architectural transparency can perform *transparently*, or whether instead it contributes to turning the buildings it clads into exclusive fortresses.

The second interesting question posed by transparency is that of its maintenance. Such expansive surfaces of clear glass require ongoing management and cleaning.[17] A building is not a rendering: it is not static, but rather a material reality that commands attention, experiences change, undergoes adaptation, and constantly transforms as well as ages—at best becoming softer over time, as everyday life renders it more human in its imperfections. To engage in maintenance that refuses to freeze architecture in its original state and intent but rather learns to adapt and embrace its weathering, unexpected uses, and adaptation is critical—not only to a building's physical longevity but also to its acceptance as a familiar, lived-in, and loved member of the built environment. It is in this sense that the maintenance of transparency extends beyond the physical properties of glass to the ongoing efforts to design and then maintain a process of communication

11
Koolhaas, *Delirious New York*, 155.

12
Colin Rowe and Robert Slutzky, "Transparency: Literal and Phenomenal," in *Perspecta* 8 (1963): 45–54.

13
Charles Belfoure, *Monuments to Money: The Architecture of American Banks* (Jefferson, NC: McFarland, 2005).

14
Reinhold Martin, "Financial Imaginaries: Toward a Philosophy of the City," *Grey Room* 42 (Winter 2011): 60–79.

15
See Bernard Tschumi, *The Manhattan Transcripts* (London: Academy Editions, 1981).

16
Reinhold Martin, "Remarks on the Production of Representation," in *The Arab City: Architecture and Representation*, ed. Amale Andraos and Nora Akawi (New York: Columbia Books on Architecture and the City, 2016).

17
Hilary Sample, *Maintenance Architecture* (Cambridge, MA: MIT Press, 2016).

Lenfest Center for the Arts abutting the Jerome L. Greene Science Center. Photograph by Tom Harris.

constructed as a constant feedback loop of exchange with the immediate community, surrounding neighborhood, broader city, and world beyond. In many ways, today's urban university campuses have a unique opportunity to act as stewards of a city's fabric, as they carve out and preserve open space, and model the increasingly rarified possibility of negotiating private functions with an investment in architecture and a commitment to their open spaces being public. The Manhattanville buildings are invited to act as diplomatic agents negotiating the relationship not only between the labs "inside" and the street "outside," but also more broadly, and as importantly, between academic and public spheres, between theory and practice, between autonomous production of new research, scholarship, and knowledge and engagement with the world—the urgent, complex,

and challenging realties all clamoring for attention.

It is not a coincidence that Piano's embrace of both the grid and of transparency exist at the intersection of conflicting possibilities, for they reflect the complexity of the changing university, suspended between the autonomy that has enabled its great freedom and sense of purpose and the realization that preserving its disengagement and isolation from the world can only lead to its irrelevance— an obsolescence that would come at devastating cost to the city, and the realities beyond its edges. As the double conditions of globalization and climate change continue to alter the order of the world and, by extension, the academic disciplines and structures of knowledge that were formed to serve it, the double pro-position of grid and glass and their hesitant porosity points to our present condition of uncertainty, inviting us to take responsibility in projecting

possibilities for the future. Architectural and urban forms always hold together the history of their past failures, as well as their past successes. The first building blocks of the Manhattanville campus expansion will only be as successful as the commitment to the ideas that have driven its vision: an architectural, urban, and academic project that is neither totally isolated nor totally connected, neither entirely autonomous nor entirely engaged, neither single-handedly top down nor exclusively bottom up. Rather, this is an ongoing project imagined as a continuous process about and for the future, a future in which the relationships that have long been constructed as opposites—inside and outside, theory and practice, the abstract and the real, campus and city—need to be reimagined and formed anew.

1916

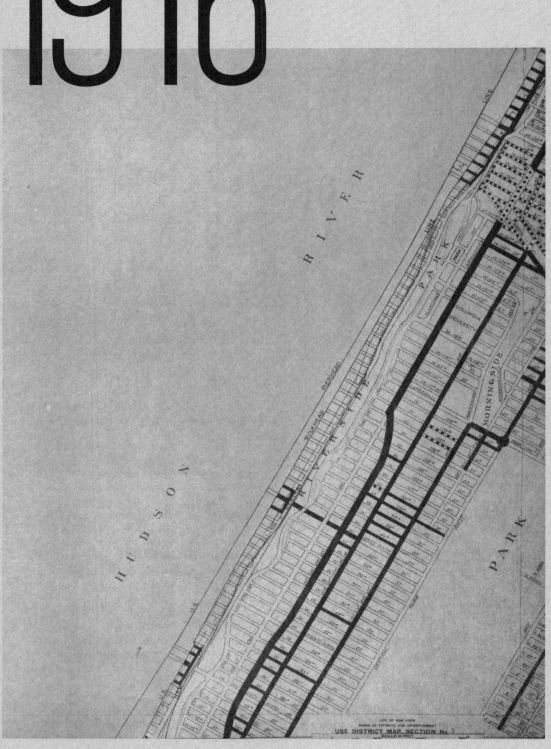

The 1916 Zoning Resolution

Known for establishing the height limits and setbacks that shaped early twentieth century skyscrapers, ensuring they would not shroud New York City streets, the 1916 Zoning Resolution also created the framework to dictate land use across the five boroughs for the first time. Its three simple classifications—residential, commercial, and manufacturing—aimed to prevent the proximity of housing and commerce to noxious areas of industry.

At that time, Manhattanville, on the Hudson's bank, had been a vibrant locus of light industry on the island for years, serviced by the 125th Street ferry terminal and the Hudson railroad line and flanked by farmland (which by 1916 was fast disappearing). The resolution cemented this use, codifying the existing assortment of tanneries, factories, breweries, and milk bottling plants as a manufacturing district, paving the way for continued industrial use. With the rise of these industries and the extension of the grid and subway lines north, the open lands and estates of pastoral Manhattanville gave way to the tenement housing erected to meet the needs of the city's fast-growing population. In the 1950s and '60s much of Manhattanville's residentially zoned blocks along Broadway would become the site of two major public housing projects—the Grant and the Manhattanville Houses.

While Manhattanville's microeconomy prospered into the 1950s, by the late 1960s manufacturing in Manhattan had declined, reducing the area to a zone of modest light industry. During those years Columbia University began moving its art studios to what had been the Sheffield milk bottling plant and offices to the former Studebaker car factory. As production moved out of the city, white-collar work in the finance and service sectors (whose offices were housed in those setback skyscrapers) became the engine of the city's economy, both elevating the need for university-educated labor and contributing to a decline in employment for former industrial workers (the consequences of which were felt most acutely in the 1970s during the city's fiscal near-collapse). Yet the 1961 Zoning Resolution, passed just before this shift, had maintained Manhattanville's manufacturing zoning, which would only be altered by the creation of the Special Manhattanville Mixed-Use District in 2007.

The gradual transformations in land use from the 1960s onward indicate New York's early turn to a knowledge economy. And perhaps it is not surprising that many decisive moments in Manhattanville's history arose in that decade—a time of tumultuous change in Harlem but also of optimism in urban planning as an agent of empowerment and social amelioration.

THE UNIVERSITY IN THE CITY
Renzo Piano in Conversation with Amale Andraos and Nicolai Ouroussoff

In March 2015, Renzo Piano spoke at Columbia University's Graduate School of Architecture, Planning, and Preservation on the master plan for the university's new Manhattanville campus (in collaboration with Skidmore, Owings & Merrill), and the design and construction of its earliest buildings—projects led by Renzo Piano Building Workshop's partner-in-charge Antoine Chaaya. In his presentation, Piano considered the form of the contemporary campus and the value of transparency. Amale Andraos and Nicolai Ouroussoff responded.

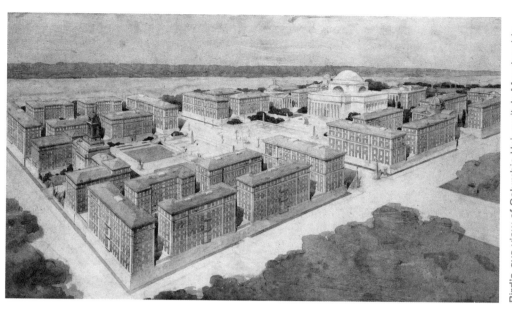

Bird's-eye view of Columbia University's Morningside Heights campus, McKim, Mead & White, 1903, watercolor on paper, Jules Crow, delineator. Courtesy of the New-York Historical Society.

Renzo Piano

Columbia sits on what is, really, a fantastic campus. Through its architecture, this school evokes a sense of community—an anomaly when you think about campus architecture in this city—and something that also elicits a certain degree of tension between Manhattan and the school. Columbia was always envisioned in relationship to New York, to the metropolis, but also apart from it. McKim, Mead & White designed it as a small acropolis, breaking from the grid with its knolls and terraces. That gesture—the use of landscape and topography—was a device intended to enclose and protect. Protection is indeed built into the history of this campus, and into a history of campus architecture. It is an understandable, at times desirable, thing. In the case of Columbia, the intent was to withdraw students from the development and the commercialization that drives so much of Manhattan and enclose them in a scholarly environment.

At the same time, this sense of productive remove creates a campus that is fundamentally guarded—it is a community, but it is not an entirely inclusionary one. The gates to Broadway and Amsterdam confer this sense of both asylum and fortification, as well as an aura of dignity that comes from history. History, after all, inheres in the formal language of McKim, Mead & White. Through classical forms and classical plans, the school invokes tradition. That's fine. It's a nice story. At one point it was even a modern story. But the story we have to tell today is different. Today we have to accept that we have to be contemporary.

Making a contemporary campus, an urban campus, is incredibly complex. And that complexity is exactly what is under way in the new campus Columbia is building in Manhattanville. Manhattanville is just a few blocks north of Morningside, on 125th Street (Martin Luther King Jr. Boulevard) and on 129th and 130th Streets, but it

17

looks entirely elsewhere. Cities transform quite quickly, but not that quickly. And in their slowness we can watch them change and watch them grow—maybe we can even learn from them. What I want to address here is urbanity, the science of challenging that, and what it means to make a modern campus.

What does it mean to be contemporary within the specific historical context of a site? The most apparent historical references in Manhattanville are from the early

twentieth century and, more recently, from the 1960s. There is Riverside Drive and the elevated subway structure. You also have Studebaker, a former milk factory to the north of 125th Street, and Prentis Hall to the south, which was once a meat-packing facility. There are also the Manhattanville and Grant Houses built by the New York Housing Authority in the 1950s early '60s and home to an active community of residents. One challenge on the site is to design an architecture that evokes a sense of dignity and unity without necessarily being guarded, without necessarily protecting, but instead by opening and making more accessible space and resources.

We have been working on this job something like fourteen years, and it's a sizable challenge. We will see the results in a few years—less than that actually—but of course it will take more time to be visible. The first building, the Jerome L. Greene Science Center, home to the Mortimer B. Zuckerman Mind Brain Behavior Institute, is almost finished now. The center is a groundbreaking research facility for neuroscience, with facilities that encourage interdisciplinary research endeavors on everything from language to memory. We are also building a new venue building for the School of the Arts and working on a conference center that is right at the connection between 125th Street and Broadway. Enclosed between these buildings will be a small piazza; though only 200 by 200 square meters, it will become an immediate destination in the neighborhood as it opens onto 125th Street.

Fundamentally this is the essence of a campus: we have science, we have art, and we have community. It is a place built around the idea of shared values and of cultivating diverse approaches to life. Typically universities are removed from the city—they are seen as refuges from the world and built apart from its quotidian freneticism. But not

18

The Sheffield Farms milk bottling plant in what is now Prentis Hall, the studio building for Columbia University's School of the Arts. Photograph from Architects' and Builders' Magazine, 1910.

only are we making a new campus in the middle of the city, we are building it in a very energetic part of the city where you have a very complex urban condition.

To build a truly contemporary campus, you have to accept that university and community must merge in some way. Security will always be an issue, but the challenge is to find creative ways to facilitate both safety and interactivity through the buildings themselves. When you work on mind, brain, and behavior, for instance, you need safe facilities, and you do need that sense of protection, especially in the laboratories, for both students and for the residents living nearby. But security is something that works better with transparency than opacity. The ground level of the Greene Science Center, for instance, is open to the public. Yes, the walls are all of glass, but that's not the only way in which we thought about transparency and articulated it through design. There will also be an installation inside the lobby, designed by the Center for Spatial Research here at GSAPP, that will communicate the research taking place throughout the building on interactive displays and will connect to activities happening in the screening room and public classroom on that level.

On 125th, 129th, 130th, Broadway, and Riverside, we have planned the flow of traffic as though the site was a little town; traffic and people will move through seamlessly, without barriers. Underground, though, is the unifying element holding everything together—the master plan. Functionally speaking, Manhattanville is incredibly different from Morningside because the plan is not broken in pieces; below grade the buildings connect and share basic infrastructure. We have one center for energy, for example, that will power every building. Parking is below grade, even

Site plan of Manhattanville and Morningside Heights campuses, Renzo Piano Building Workshop and David Brody Bond Aedas, 2009. Courtesy of Renzo Piano Building Workshop.

lab and classroom space. Everything is working like one unit. Underground there's continuity between the various campus buildings, but on ground the buildings also belong to the city.

The campus is a deft synthesis of public and private spaces. The Lenfest Center for the School of the Arts is an excellent example. It has both open performance spaces and other academic spaces. Primarily, of course, the campus is about teaching and about learning, but the street level is going to be vastly public, with a program that is both inherent to each school and that invites in the community and city at large. The art gallery, for example, will be on the ground floor. The same openness you see in the Lenfest Center is also true of the Mind Brain Behavior Institute building. It's an incredibly complex research center, and we wanted to make that accessible, and legible, to anyone who might visit the facility, for whatever purpose, including that ground-level classroom available for educational activities to teach schoolchildren in West Harlem about the brain.

The dialogue between these two buildings is what makes this campus so dynamic: art and science side by side. Art is there not just because the school needs a venue for performance but also because art adds another dimension, even in a little campus. Art makes people more cultivated and more complex. Art provokes wonder in people, and science does the same. So at the center level, art and science meet. They are the same desire, and they build desire, a desire based in curiosity and experimentation. This was the idea in the beginning. Of course the campus will grow, but this is what will open over the next couple of years.

Amale Andraos The openness of your architecture is very literal. The corners don't meet, and it remains incomplete. This invokes a sense of generosity in the blurring of inside and out. I was curious how that translates from architecture to master plan. You think fundamentally as an architect, so what was the difference, or what were the challenges, in translating that building-scale approach to the master plan?

R P You grow up with this funny idea that architecture and city are the same thing—they merge. You cannot think about building without thinking about the relationship to the street and to the rest of the world. It's built into the DNA of the architect. At the end of the day, I don't think what we do is so complicated. Typically what we do—the Manhattanville campus included—we try to make a building fly. It's not a joke. A building can fly, but it needs a little column somewhere, a little lift or a push, as it were. The idea is that you don't occupy the land where the building is, and in this way you give back to the city what the city gave to you—space.

21

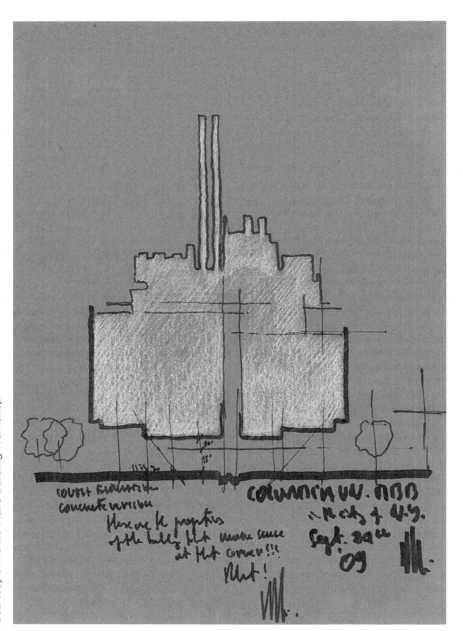

What I love most about the early sketches of a building is that it is not architecture; rather, it is the promise of architecture. We don't have big ideas. Every project, to an extent, shares the same goals, the same desires, but it's never the same thing because of course, thank God, the projects are different, they never manifest in the same way. And what we are doing at Columbia is this: the first three buildings, the Jerome L. Greene Science Center, the Lenfest Center, and the conference center, fly. Of course they touch ground, but the ground floor is public and open; it's permeable, it's porous, and it's accessible. I cannot see a frontier between a building, a city, and the street. This is the real secret of making buildings that are loved and are adopted, because they are not selfish. This idea of creating a place where the city and the building meet is maybe a bit simplified—typically it's not easy. But normally the earth is not that stable; normally it moves. We have earthquakes. So to make a building that flies means that you have to bring forces down to ground.

Nicolai Ouroussoff   This tension between flying and grounding is more difficult than it seems. When I had the privilege of actually working in a Renzo Piano building (the New York Times Building), what I admired the most about the building was the way that it meets the ground. There's a beautiful visual sequence from Eighth Avenue where you look through the lobby, through the auditorium, through a courtyard, and over the stage to the seats. So when you're sitting in the seats in the auditorium, you're looking both at the stage and through the courtyard, through the lobby and back out into the city. It's a beautiful experience, and there is a social idea motivating it, which is public porosity. The Times Building was built at a moment, soon after 2001, when the paper felt as though it was a potential target of terrorism, so there were very heated discussions internally about whether such openness was prudent or possible.

R P   That's proof that urban design and what I call magic come together. The multiple plane, and the view through it, was something we were very conscious of creating. When we were working on the New York Times Building, we sat so many times in the auditorium looking through the stage, looking through the garden, looking through the lobby, and looking to the traffic on the street. The transparency becomes a visible expression of complexity and belonging, because the building is not just an object, it is a system. This is part of what I call language. It's not style—it has nothing to do with style. It is simply predicated on creating urban complexity.

23

NO   This idea of openness, it's a reimagining of the Morningside campus. But there's another thing about the Manhattanville project that I was drawn to from early on, which was that it has a completely unified language. The default position of developers now for a while has been when you do a large-scale development you gather many different architects who work in different styles and piece them together. There is an element of camouflage in that approach I think—this artificial idea of difference that belies the homogeneity generated by the control of a central economic entity. One of the things I find interesting about the campus is that in that language and the continuity of that language, one hears an echo of a period when modernism still had the possibility of giving us a sense of common purpose, which I think has fragmented in the last thirty years.

It is not just that you took away the walls and integrated the master plan into the grid and lifted up all the ground but rather that all of the buildings are designed in the same language. There's a sense of unity, even as you're opening up. While I know that different architects will eventually build in the campus, the comprehensive master plan and the coherence of your first three buildings distinguish the campus from other large-scale projects going up in Manhattan—Hudson Yards, for instance. It's a platform that will allow different strands of a formal language to emerge, and to resonate, in the future.

RP   Yes, these different strands of language will of course emerge. We designed those original three buildings, and other buildings will be designed by the other architects working on the site in the future—Diller Scofidio + Renfro and FXFOWLE, to name two. The sense of unity doesn't mean uniformity. Unity is good, uniformity is bad. I think you are quite right. Sometimes it's a bit overused, this idea that you call many people all together so this becomes more interesting. It's like mimicking history. The reason why cities are beautiful is because they are really built in different moments by different people, by different architects, by different desires, by different lives.

That's the reason why when you look at the city, it's so beautiful. When you go up on the Empire State Building and you look down, or in Rome you go up on one of the hills, you look down, you realize that the beauty is the fact that those cities are the mirror of millions of lives, and there are millions of different lives unfolding in them. Diversity is part of that. When you try to mimic that diversity, the effect is not the same.

We are not going to be designing buildings for Columbia University forever. I think we will be very happy if we can actually make Phase One work well. The Jerome L. Greene Science Center is different from the Lenfest Center, which is different from the conference center, simply because they serve completely different functions. The Science Center is a kind of urban machine, a soft machine, a gentle machine—very transparent. It will not look at all like a corporate building, that's for sure. It's not a corporate building, it's something else—a factory perhaps.

When you go to the Lenfest Center, it's like a little, brave David—it's solid. Inside we have a performance theater, a movie theater, and other similar functions. Light is projected from the top. It's different from the activities of the mind, brain, and behavior research in the Science Center. It's actually different by necessity, inevitably different.

Uniformity comes when you do something like office blocks and they are doing the same thing. One is equal to the other. Because those three buildings are so different, I don't think we are running any risk to become uniform. And I hope we do what you say, that a certain unity comes out from the fact that they are different but they speak with the same language.

N O In your New York work though there is almost a uniformity of approach and language in a way that you don't see as much in your European work. And I wonder if that has to do with Manhattan? It kind of moves in a more Miesian direction.

R P You know, Nicolai, I'm not that intelligent. Architecture is a funny profession because you become the city where you go to work. We were working in the office for a long time in Berlin, and we became Berliners. It was difficult to become Japanese in Japan, but we tried. In some way you absorb. You cannot be an architect like a tourist. You have to be part of the city. You have to understand the city. So probably what you say is correct. If you work in Malta in the middle of the Mediterranean Sea, it's about light. It's about the sky. So the inspiration comes of course from client, from function, but it comes also from the place.

Today I can't see any difference between searching for beauty or dreaming about poetry and working on light or inventing a piece of a joint for observing the site and measuring things— all these come together.

Sketch for the Lenfest Center for the Arts, Renzo Piano Building Workshop, 2013. Courtesy of Renzo Piano Building Workshop.

At nine o'clock you are a poet. At ten you are a builder. At eleven you become a social worker. At midday normally you protest, and then you have lunch. I suspect that everybody brings with them the memories that make you what you are. But then as an architect, you have to accept that you react in a different way, and you have to be loyal in that. You have to be honest. You cannot pretend. In Manhattan, in New York, you are a New Yorker.

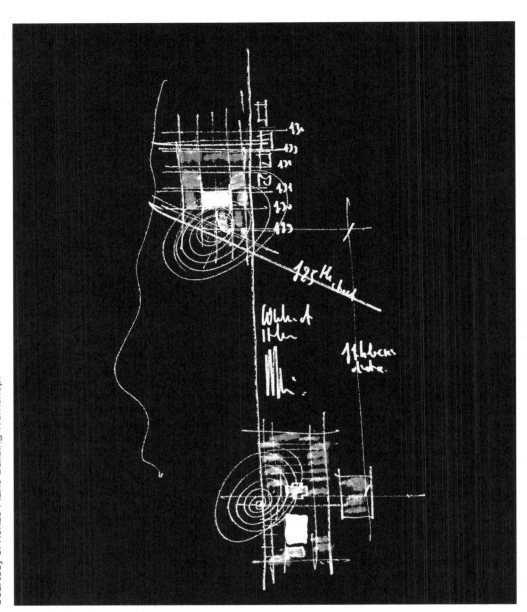

Manhattanville campus master plan sketch, Renzo Piano Building Workshop, 2004.
Courtesy of Renzo Piano Building Workshop.

AA   In your mind, what does Manhattanville say about the kinds of transformation the university is going through? I don't mean just Columbia, but in general—the push toward research or the programs represented in the kind of buildings that are going up in Manhattanville? In your mind, like if you look at Morningside and then you look at Manhattanville, how would you interpret that change we are experiencing?

RP   There have been few moments more transformational for the university, in my mind, than the one we are in now. Everywhere universities are expanding, but they do not expand in the same ways. There are different models around the world—branch campuses or whole city sectors built up around education and populated with the outposts of American institutions in Asia and the Middle East. There are also different models in New York City; one only need look downtown to see that.

For architecture this new drive to build presents many opportunities, of course, but they are opportunities we have to consider carefully. For me, the question is: what will the role of the university be in the city? And also, what are the changes happening in education right now, and how are they implemented through campus architecture? And it is for precisely these reasons that I find it remarkable that Columbia is building in Manhattanville. The school is staying uptown, and it is staying urban. Manhattanville doesn't just look south to Morningside, it also looks north to the Medical School on 168th Street and, along with these two campuses, I think will be an important part of the university's presence in Harlem.

Importantly, this project is also a commitment to a serious scope of research. I meant what I said about the intersection of science and art. It's a very potent kind of disciplinary collision, and one that is becoming increasingly rare as new campuses silo the sciences from the arts or even the liberal arts. Architecture can quite literally remedy such a divide, but this doesn't mean that we aren't without our own set of concerns or responsibilities to this context. Architecture ought to engineer the spaces of novel encounters, to uphold the traditional cultural necessity of an institution like Columbia and allow that institution to transform according to the dynamic needs of a city and the ever-changing landscape of knowledge.

When Columbia first moved its campus to Morningside over one hundred years ago, the school was in a not entirely dissimilar position. I think the question at that time was how to make a campus that engaged its metropolitan condition, and how to provide space for rigorous scientific research and new modes of practice in the sciences. Yet if the questions are similar, the responses to those questions have changed significantly. It once sufficed to open an axis between the street and the campus, to provide relief from the grid with green lawns and contemplative quadrangles. And Columbia's campus is great—these are real gifts to the city and to the students. But now the task of architecture is not only to facilitate discovery and interdisciplinary work; it is also to invite the public into that work, to make it legible, to make the school into a citizen too.

27

1961

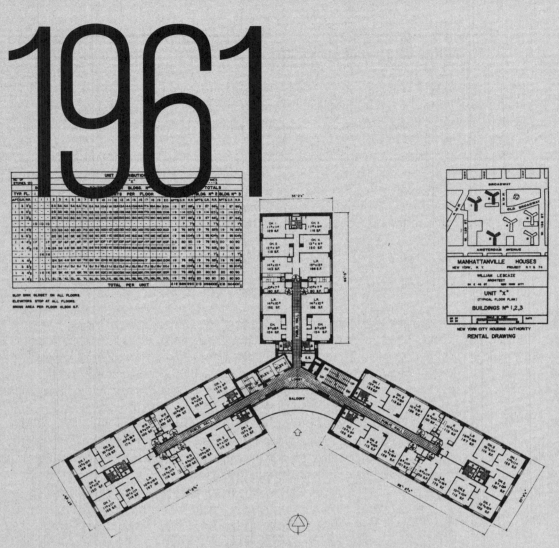

Typical floor plan for Manhattanville Houses
1, 2, and 3, William Lescaze, 1954. Copyright
of the New York City Housing Authority.

Manhattanville Houses under construction,
March 1960. Copyright of the New York City
Housing Authority.

The Manhattanville Houses

The Manhattanville Houses opened in the summer of 1961. Designed by William Lescaze—a Swiss architect well known for his work on postwar housing and for his commitment to the aesthetic and social elements of European modernism—they spanned a superblock bound by 126th and 133rd Streets between Broadway and Amsterdam; six twenty-story buildings housed 1,272 apartments. Built as public housing construction in New York City was beginning to wane, this "state-aided low-rent housing project" aimed to attract an "enlivened tenant body interested in good living, good schools, and forward looking community" and, accordingly, included a gymnasium, day care, and health centers for both children and adults and a community center with recreational programs, vocational counseling, and cultural events.[1]

More than a decade before, the cultural institutions of Morningside Heights (its universities, churches, synagogues, and hospitals) had banded together to form Morningside Heights Inc., a nonprofit organization dedicated to, as their literature stated, "turning back the tide of deterioration which they saw sweeping the neighborhood"—the product of the suburban exodus of the middle class, deteriorating housing (at the time 90 percent of housing in Harlem was over thirty years old and much was over fifty),

and increased crime.[2] The group advocated for "honest-to-goodness, unsegregated, interracial housing," a desire that would lay the foundation for the future Manhattanville and Grant housing projects.[3] In 1949, the Federal Housing Act allocated funds to assist municipalities in buying and clearing slum tenements (Title I of the act) as well as building low-rent public housing (Title III). In Manhattanville, following encouragement from Morningside Heights Inc., the city purchased and cleared the parcel stretching between 133rd and 126th Streets and transferred the land to the New York City Housing Authority (NYCHA), which covered the streets and began the process of building in 1958.

Lescaze, who had designed NYCHA's Ten Eyck (now Williamsburg) Houses in Brooklyn in 1938 and whose proposed design for housing between Chrystie and Forsyth Streets displayed at the Museum of Modern Art in 1932 was influential in the social housing conversation in New York City, deployed the chevron shape—a configuration that had by then become a popular typology in public housing—to create apartments with maximal light and ventilation and enclose public areas, ensuring optimal spaces for modern living. Rent for these apartments ranged from $51 to $110 monthly, including utilities. For a one-bedroom, the maximum

income would have been just shy of $4,000 annually, and for families it was a hair under $8,000.

Thirteen years after the Manhattanville Houses opened—as the city inched toward bankruptcy—tenants waged a rent strike, protesting the broken elevators, lack of maintenance, and the rising rents. NYCHA's inability to address these concerns exacerbated rising crime in the houses, fostering an embittered relationship with the police, which continues into the present (in 2014, the NYPD raided the Manhattanville and adjacent Grant Houses searching for gang members). Yet many of the early residents still live in Manhattanville Houses, and the tenants associations were active in conversations around the 2007 Special Manhattanville Mixed-Use District rezoning and the formulation of Community Board 9's alternative zoning proposal.

1
Petition of the New York City Housing Authority to the Board of Estimate of New York City, December 2, 1955, Box 0073D2, Folder 06, and Project Resources Information, Box 0065D8, Folder 05, both in New York City Housing Authority Collection, LaGuardia and Wagner Archives, Long Island City, NY.

2
Margaret Boulton Bartlett, *Morningside Manhattanville: A Pioneering Urban Redevelop-ment Program* (New York: Morningside Heights Inc., 1953), 2. For statistics on housing, see June Meyer Jordan, "Instant Slum Clearance," *Esquire*, April 1965, 110.

3
Bartlett, *Morningside Manhattanville*, 2.

MASTER PLANNERS AS NEW YORKERS

An Interview with Marilyn Taylor, Anthony Vacchione, Lois Mazzitelli, and Philip Palmgren

In 2002, architecture, interior design, engineering, and urban planning firm Skidmore, Owings & Merrill (SOM) was engaged to work on the master plan for Columbia University's campus expansion. In the following interview with editor Caitlin Blanchfield, the project's leaders, Marilyn Taylor, Anthony Vacchione, Lois Mazzitelli, and Philip Palmgren, discuss the Manhattanville site, working with both city and community, and the collaborative design process.

Let's start at the beginning.
How did the design process begin?

Anthony Vacchione   When we started this project, back in 2005, the memory of 1968 was still very palpable—of Columbia trying to put a gym in Morningside Park, and of the property that the university had been accumulating since the mid-1960s to stabilize this neighborhood. There was still a cloud hanging over this area of Manhattan's West Side.

It arose in the 1960s when the university decided to stay in Morningside Heights, having considered moving to Westchester or other places because of the deterioration of the neighborhood. Three decades later, it had become apparent that Columbia was facing a very different problem: as an urban university, it had far less square footage per student than other comparable schools, which was a concern in terms of long-term competitiveness. What our team at SOM was retained to do included a series of studies to look once again at alternate sites for growth, of which West Manhattanville was one.

Marilyn Taylor   When we started our work, there was a lot of tension in the Manhattanville neighborhood, as well as deep feelings about environmental justice. It was not directed to Columbia alone but also to the industrial uses and the bus repair facility located in a block along 133rd Street between Broadway and Twelfth Avenue. Community members were well informed about air pollutants and a concentration of asthma among their children; they felt that their important concerns were not being heard.

At the beginning of our work to define strategies for additional space at Columbia, we first looked at the East Campus, identifying improvements to create a better setting through changes to the Law School, the School of International and Public Affairs, and the housing tower on the west edge of the Morningside Park. But after months of study—by the time Lee Bollinger arrived as president—Columbia's attention had turned to the potential of Manhattanville and the blocks immediately north of 125th Street, between Broadway and Twelfth Avenue, beneath an elevated portion of the West Side Highway. At that time, the blocks were mostly industrial.

31

Philip Palmgren One of the first things I remember after that analysis was going to the Columbia Trustees meeting and presenting the initial plan.

M T The preliminary master plan concepts we had developed at that point took a very public approach to the ways in which Columbia might extend its presence to Manhattanville, specifically the sites between West 125th and West 133rd Streets. The early concepts proposed that the Manhattan street grid would be maintained, with all existing crosstown streets remaining open as public streets—no superblocks!—and with public spaces introduced into the mid-blocks, breaking down the scale of development and making the entire campus open to everyone in the neighborhood. During this time, we worked with a number of community representatives to create a framework of compatibility and interaction with Manhattanville.

A V Early on, we realized it was necessary to split the blocks in half—much like they did at Rockefeller Center— to make them more manageable.

M T When Lee Bollinger became president, he was very interested in building a design team who would not only define a groundbreaking public-oriented master plan but also illustrate the site's potential with architectural concepts that shared the public orientation and respected the qualities of Manhattanville. Tony and I remember getting a phone call inquiring about the possibility of teaming up with Renzo Piano Building Workshop (RPBW). It seemed like a great idea for working together to give the campus both variety in architecture as well as a strong public realm.

And at that point was the master plan mostly completed?

M T The answer is yes, and no—as it always is in New York City. We had been through a process of validating the principles that we'd originally talked about: streets that are open, walkable, and pedestrian-oriented to encourage everyone to use and enjoy them; a variety of buildings meeting the streets in a welcoming way; and improvements to connections between the inland communities and the Hudson River. It was going to be necessary to have parking, but it would be—at greater expense—underground. At the same time, the plan would take advantage of its closeness to the 125th Street subway station, a historic and iconic elevated structure elegantly spanning the valley between Morningside Heights and 133rd Street, creating a new public transit-oriented destination. The plans, sections, and elevations suggested a university

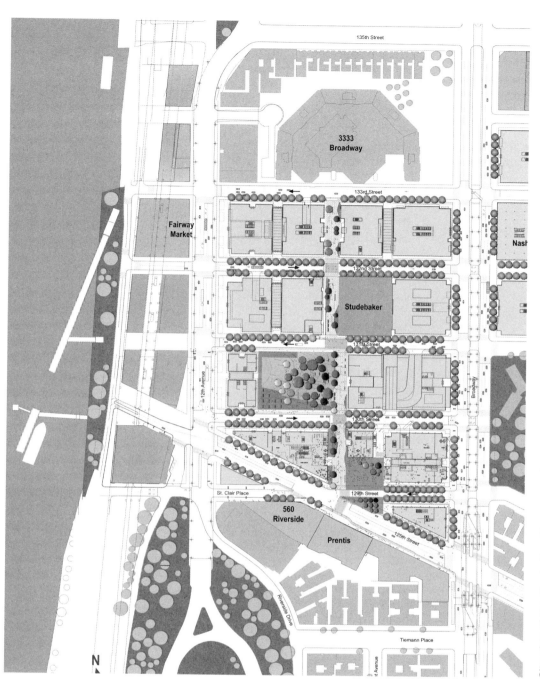

135th Street

3333
Broadway

133rd Street

Fairway
Market

Nash

132nd Street

Studebaker

131st Street

12th Avenue

Broadway

130th Street

129th Street

St. Clair Place

125th Street

560
Riverside

Prentis

Riverside Drive

Tiemann Place

N

Site plan of the Manhattanville campus. Courtesy of SOM and Renzo Piano Building Workshop.

district very different from the classical one at 116th Street—open to the public all the time: no walls, no barriers. And in order to make this place feel truly public, we proposed the "public layer" on the street level of the buildings, with uses including shops and cafés on the ground floor, as well as access to Columbia galleries and libraries.

One of the evolutions as the master plan moved forward was that university buildings, and lab buildings in particular, require security. But within that constraint the basic idea was that the whole ground plane of this project was open, transparent—not the solid masonry walls of the neoclassic academy building but rather an expression of modernism and inclusion.

The idea of the transparent urban layer and the public street was, and will be, extended into the ground floors of the academic buildings. At the same time, access to the upper floors, where scientific and medical research would be under way, perhaps including study of infectious disease, would be limited.

P P   Columbia's research program was a big community outreach problem. Neighbors were afraid that there were going to be infectious disease labs here, and the university had to come out and clarify the limitations and safety procedures they would include.

You always think of security as the inverse of that scenario, that students need to be secured in the university buildings. It's important to note that the community felt the need to be secured from what might be happening in the schools.

P P   I think it goes back to what Marilyn was saying about how residents in this part of Harlem felt that they were holding a huge share of the infrastructural burden in the city. They had the MTA bus depot. They had the loud subway tracks overhead. And so they felt like Columbia was potentially inserting another threatening element into their neighborhood. The challenge was to figure out how to overcome that misconception and to engage in dialogue about ways Columbia could work with the community to help with the noise of the elevated subway trains, with the emissions from the bus depot, with the Con Ed facility just across the street.

In terms of design moves, what was done to facilitate more connectivity with surrounding housing in Harlem, and with the existing urban fabric?

M T   One primary thing was to identify with the river. For instance, we made proposals for a ferry service that community members and Columbia professors, students, and visitors could use to travel between 125th and points in Midtown and Downtown Manhattan.

A V   We also looked at how Metro-North commuter lines could connect here. There's a potential that someday Metro-North could come through Penn Station and have a stop in Manhattanville, which would be a great benefit to the community as well as to the university.

P P   The community wanted to understand that the park along the Hudson at 125th Street would be their park, so Columbia agreed with their request to open up toward the park along an active and revitalized Twelfth Avenue.

A V   For so many years the university had been seen as an aggressive buyer of property. The potential of being contributing neighbors was now being put on the table.

M T   The Manhattanville Houses, across Broadway from the sites on which Columbia was proposing to build, are a New York City public housing project, which was, at the time it was built, one of the great examples of providing affordable living for lower-income New Yorkers. They're well run and have a strong tenant structure, with long-term residents. In our many public meetings at the community board, whose office was on 125th Street, we met a great many residents with many different views. Many wanted to work together with Columbia, but there was also intense community opposition.

The team at RPBW brought great design ideas to add to the master plan and urban design process. As New Yorkers, the urban designers and architects at SOM were able to bring in the local and community perspectives. We had an understanding of the approval process through which the design—including the public space so important to its success—could be realized.

35

AV   Working with the community board, the Department of City Planning, and the city council requires a focus on details as well as big ideas. For example, we had to explore how we were going to service new buildings while maintaining the width and character of Manhattan's crosstown streets. In the Morningside campus of nearly a hundred years ago, McKim, Mead & White ingeniously put together a large, below grade system of corridors, with Low Library extending out to Avery Hall and to Uris Hall. That was a huge invention, that everything can be serviced from below to create this significant, monumental building complex. Could we do the same in Manhattanville, at the neighborhood scale?

We had worked extensively with Disney, and with Disney everything disappears. It's magic. So that was the other thing that we started exploring: how to tie all this below grade so you could service everything, and then also to accommodate all the parking that we knew was going to be a requirement of the site.

We both needed to preserve what Marilyn talked about, which is this big, wonderful, open campus that was fully accessible and pedestrian-oriented, as well as integrate all the things you have in a university facility: central energy plant, parking garages, and other things that are interruptive.

P P   All the science buildings are connected below grade. The below-grade space was planned to be seven layers deep, providing service spaces for multiple uses without adversely impacting the street-level character.

How does the master plan accommodate growth and difference while also creating the framework to allow not uniformity necessarily but rather cohesiveness and connectivity?

Lois Mazzitelli   We developed a concept of building envelopes that could accommodate the required square footage while still allowing variation. This was embedded in a special zoning district that set forth parameters by which all buildings would be built within the total allowable square feet.

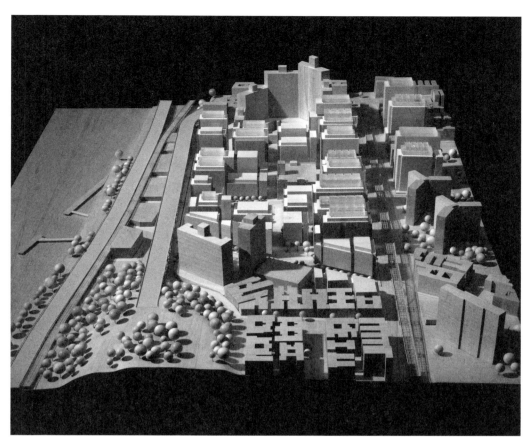

A wooden model that illustrates the future build-out and building envelopes of the master plan. Courtesy of SOM and Renzo Piano Building Workshop.

PP   I have such great memories of Marilyn and Lois talking about how big the "sweater" (our term for the building envelopes) was going to be for each of the buildings. We defined the envelope that each of these buildings could sit in and worked out a flexible system to allow the university to achieve the floor-area ratio they proposed without uniformity among all the buildings. We were trying to make the sweaters bigger to allow the university necessary flexibility as, one after another, the individual buildings came into place.

LM   On the flip side, we had to bring this model to the community as well and then try to explain to them that this is the absolute maximum envelope and that what would actually get built would be significantly smaller. For instance, the RPBW building there now is actually much smaller than the envelope that was allowed.

37

A V The community was very concerned. They didn't
want to end up with big tall buildings that cast
more shadows on them. They also wanted to
make sure that buildings weren't going to be built across the
streets, that we were going to keep these avenues open to
view the Hudson River.

I'm sure you've been down 125th Street. Today
when you are at Broadway and 125th Street and looking
toward the Hudson River, Broadway looks like a multilane,
high-capacity highway. We worked together to make it an
urban street, a pedestrian-oriented corridor bringing people
to and from the Hudson River Park. It was not a design issue;
it was an environmental impact issue, and the master plan
was able to respond through traffic planning to reduce
congestion, as well as providing a strong public space plan.

M T The most important issues rose to the top.
Community members, including those in the
Manhattanville Houses, were really concerned
that this was going to drive the price of housing sky high.
Gentrification was a huge problem then, and it's only
gotten worse in our city. Residents were concerned that
related uses would push them out, that, as we heard
almost every place we went in those days, "My children
won't be able to live in any room that they grew up in."
And there are many multigenerational families living in
the housing around the site.

As we said earlier, they felt challenged by the
MTA bus facility and the concentration of air pollutants
impacting their neighborhood. So to the extent that they
believed the plan for Manhattanville and the commitment
of Columbia would help them in those issues—not just
pushing the bus facility to move but also shifting to more
energy-efficient buses, switching to compressed natural
gas—they sought ways in which they and Columbia
could work together.

A V We pushed ourselves to look at each one of the
proposed blocks and buildings and at how
different types of labs would work. We looked at
residential alternatives. We looked at classroom buildings
and what they might be like in future decades. We studied
all different building types to gain flexibility in how the sites
can be developed in the future while remaining consistent
with the limitations of the site. We didn't want to leave the
university with a plan that didn't have the types of footprints
that would accommodate the types of uses that we know
today and some foresight of what might happen in the future.
That's what makes planning and urban design even more
difficult. But we wanted to make sure that this plan satisfied
long-term needs.

MT   Working closely with the Columbia team, especially Robert Kasdin and Maxine Griffith, we set out a plan for open and broad community interaction. We and RPBW were a team, but being local was essential. There were two or three meetings a day that were dealing with community issues. As design collaborators, we agreed on principle; SOM focused on the planning, urban design, and approvals; RPBW continued to show the vision for the architecture and its materiality and vocabulary.

AV   Manhattanville is one example of a recent shift in development in New York whereby peripheral lands around Manhattan are put to a higher use through large-scale plans. These lands were of little value to the city for many, many years because we had places, elbow room, to expand. Now that we don't have that ability, these lands suddenly have become of value. The question is: how do you integrate them back into the city? You could end up with a Tudor City, where it just turns itself away from the river. Or you could have the Manhattanville plan—open, shared, centered on the public character of the ground plane. As land becomes scarcer and scarcer there is good reason to ensure that those things that don't require a ground plane are put below grade, thus allowing the ground plane to be occupied by uses that really benefit everyone.

What were the major moves that you made below grade to free up space on the ground plane?

PP   There is a loop that connects all of these facilities to the centralized power plant and that actually tucks underneath that vivarium. In the below-grade factory you have the athletic facility and the pool. You have parking at this level. You have the loading dock. And all of these things are about thinking of a larger picture, a singular picture of systems where one benefits the next. So it's actually creating a symbiotic relationship between all the buildings and making them all function as a single sort of entity.

AV   We wanted to keep the exact topography of the site. If you think about Columbia University, a community-wide plan is brilliant. McKim, Mead & White brought the big stairs up in front of Low Library and then leveled out, causing a wall along 118th Street, and that's how they created their below grade system. Here we had a different problem: we had to use a warped surface.

P P   There is a cliff of bedrock down below, which creates a bathtub. Negotiating between a sloped ground plane and the bedrock and nothing below was actually a huge challenge to the overall planning. We were involved in the whole World Trade site, which began to overlap with this. It's exactly the same thing: another case where you've got to solve the below grade issue. Now, there it was absolutely for security. What we wanted to be sure to do was set the stage—before people had recovered and were ready to start putting shovels back in the ground to build things, not just to take the terrible, horrible stuff away—was to push that bathtub back down the grade for the same reason: so the streets could run through. And then Westfield came in, and they wanted to overwrite the streets and put in a great big shopping center. And we were able to be influential in saying, "Not in New York."

M T   It is the great urban grid of New York City that allows the city to be so democratic and inclusive. We don't have very many walled compounds here. We really are an open and free place, punctured by the subway, which means that you have effusions of people coming out even when it's not convenient for them to come out there, because that's the way our city works. And I feel like for our decades here we have worked steadily on that. Penn Station, that station's exactly the same problem.

So how will this project impact the surrounding neighborhood?

M T   From our perspective, the success strategy started when City Councilman Robert Jackson came to the meetings, and he began to understand why this would be good for the neighborhood. And Scott Stringer made the ball move as Manhattan Borough President. He went to the community, and he said, as we remember it, "You're not going to stop gentrification by stopping Columbia. I will work with you on the housing plan for this neighborhood."

P P   And then the community set forth their own ideas for this site, many of which we then incorporated into the plan that achieved city approval.

M T   It's important, I think, to put the West Manhattanville project in the context of changing Harlem. As we began our work with Columbia, the process of gentrification was well under way. The New York City Housing Partnership was working in Harlem, assembling vacant and disinvested properties and finding local developers and builders to return them to use. Harlem was beginning to attract new housing and to add retail to serve a changing community. New projects were beginning along West 125th Street in recognition of the fact that there was economic power in this community that shouldn't be flowing out. The Columbia team responded with analysis and proposed programs to keep local restaurants and local businesses in the community.

Maintaining public housing together with building new affordable and market-rate units was already becoming a big challenge for New York. I think you can see in Harlem in general, and West Harlem in particular, the ways to accomplish significant change that is integral to the neighborhood and inclusive of its existing residents as well as of the new uses that development will bring.

And, let's remember, universities like Columbia are very different now than they were in the days when the Morningside Heights campus was built. One after another, American universities are engaging in sharing responsibilities with the communities they are situated in. Columbia's plan is an example of how to offer jobs and extend access to education. We think there's a lot to be said about this evolution of the university. And there are very few institutions that have such a clear example of one campus from a hundred years ago and another that's for the twenty-first century only a few blocks apart.

Columbia's investment in West Manhattanville is a bold commitment to the belief that place is still going to matter for a university. But if you think about it from another perspective, West Manhattanville may well be the place that gives Columbia the opportunity to experiment, have different forms of education, and relate much more with the community, and with the whole world, since we're brought closer through the media and the global trade of goods, resources, and ideas. And in the New York context, we literally talked about how it'll be easier for people to visit Manhattanville than Morningside. It's easier than getting to 116th Street to come up here on Metro-North or on a ferry. This is a place to be. It can be a physical place, but it really stands for something else now.

A V   These issues of how the university, community, and access to education interrelate—and of how design supports that, enhances it, ennobles it, and even makes it an experience that we all enjoy—these are fundamental issues where planners and designers, with future-oriented clients like the Columbia leadership, can indeed make a difference.

1964

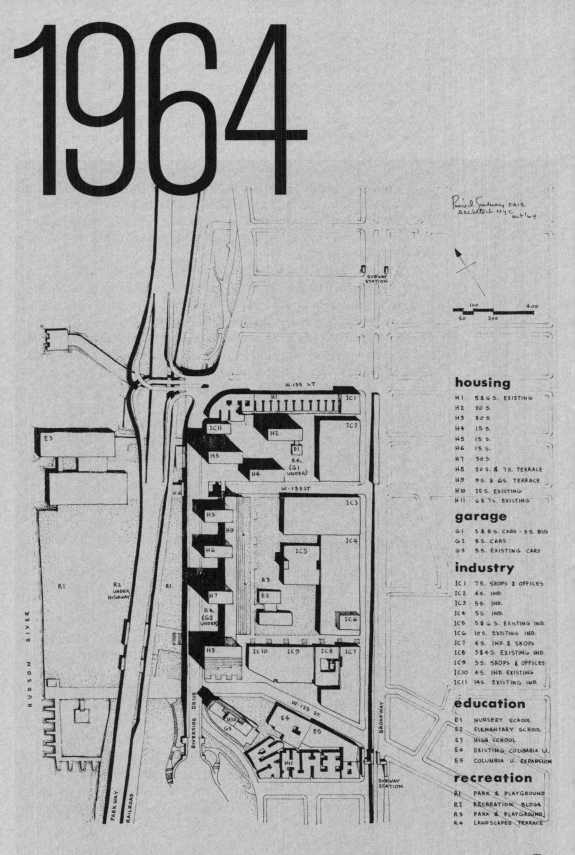

Percival Goodman F.A.I.A.
Architect N.Y.C. Oct '64

SUBWAY
STATION

W.135 ST

W.133 ST

W.125 ST

SUBWAY
STATION

HUDSON RIVER

PARKWAY

RAILROAD

RIVERSIDE DRIVE

BROADWAY

housing

H1	5 & 6 S. EXISTING
H2	20 S.
H3	30 S.
H4	15 S.
H5	15 S.
H6	15 S.
H7	30 S.
H8	20 S. & 7 S. TERRACE
H9	9 S. & 6 S. TERRACE
H10	25 S. EXISTING
H11	6 & 7 S. EXISTING

garage

G1	5 & 6 S. CARS - 3 S. BUS
G2	8 S. CARS
G3	5 S. EXISTING CARS

industry

IC1	7 S. SHOPS & OFFICES
IC2	4 S. IND.
IC3	5 S. IND.
IC4	5 S. IND.
IC5	5 & 6 S. EXISTING IND.
IC6	10 S. EXISTING IND.
IC7	4 S. IND. & SHOPS
IC8	3 & 4 S. EXISTING IND.
IC9	3 S. SHOPS & OFFICES
IC10	4 S. IND. EXISTING
IC11	14 S. EXISTING IND.

education

E1	NURSERY SCHOOL
E2	ELEMENTARY SCHOOL
E3	HIGH SCHOOL
E4	EXISTING COLUMBIA U.
E5	COLUMBIA U. EXPANSION

recreation

R1	PARK & PLAYGROUND
R2	RECREATION BLDGS
R3	PARK & PLAYGROUND
R4	LANDSCAPED TERRACE

SITE PLAN

1

M on H

Plan drawing of Manhattanville-on-Hudson, Percival
Goodman, 1964. Courtesy of Avery Architectural
& Fine Arts Library, Columbia University.

Manhattanville-on-Hudson

Approached by a West Harlem neighborhood group exploring prospects of urban renewal in the area, architect Percival Goodman developed a mixed-use plan for the Manhattanville neighborhood as part of an urban planning studio he was teaching at Columbia University's Graduate School of Architecture and Planning in the fall of 1964. Called Manhattanville-on-Hudson, the plan—which occupied a nearly identical footprint to the current Manhattanville campus—included middle- and low-income housing, parks, playgrounds, and recreational facilities, and office and retail space alongside existing light industry, a nursery school, an elementary school, a high school, and one additional Columbia University building next to the art studios in Prentis Hall. Drawings show fields and open green space extending under the Twelfth Avenue viaduct and a raised freeway along the Hudson River. Schools were placed across from terraced housing towers enclosing a park. A marina accommodated small boats.

Four years before, Goodman had co-written *Communitas* with his brother, the sociologist Paul Goodman. It was a socially minded treatise on architecture and urbanism that advocated for density, the close proximity of one's home and place of work, public art, planning at the neighborhood scale, and urban design for public good. Situated between the massive-scaled utopian plans of figures like Le Corbusier and the neighborhood advocacy of urbanists like Jane Jacobs, Goodman's work encapsulated a strain of advocacy planning emerging in the 1960s.

The Manhattanville-on-Hudson plan included housing subsidies for low-income residents to be able to afford the middle-income apartments the plan proposed. When Goodman offered Morningside Heights Inc.—an organization of local institutions including Columbia University—as a potential sponsor of the project, he was met with opposition from residents who feared that any university influence would result in housing for only middle- and high-income people, excluding many who already lived in and around Manhattanville, one of the broader fears concerning urban renewal at the time (and still today). The proposal, which was a response to a solicitation by the Manhattanville Urban Renewal Study Committee, never moved forward, though many of its elements would resurface years later in an alternate proposal for Manhattanville put together by Community Board 9.

HELICAL BUILDING
An Interview with Elizabeth Diller and Charles Renfro

Diller Scofidio + Renfro were commissioned to design the new facilities for the Columbia Business School, which will be housed in two buildings between 130th and 131st Streets, and Broadway and Twelfth Avenue. Though ground has only just broken on these structures, they represent the first of the second phase of construction in Manhattanville, and a new design voice within the master plan. In the following interview with editor Caitlin Blanchfield, Elizabeth Diller, and Charles Renfro discuss designing for twenty-first century pedagogy, helical circulation, and Fred and Ginger.

I'd like to begin with your design process. How did you conceive of the concept for the new Columbia Business School building?

Charles Renfro

The pedagogy of the business school depends on very close student, faculty, and administration interaction. We didn't want this to be a place where the faculty sat at the top and the students were consigned to the base of the building. Our first strategy was to comb these two populations together in order to encourage collaboration and unpredictable interaction between the teachers and the students.

We were also interested in breaking down the programmatic hierarchies of the social and public spaces of a traditional graduate school facility. Typically, student lounges and dining facilities are stand-alone spaces. We envisioned these programs as the glue—the goo, you might say—that would spread between the more precisely defined program elements so that whenever someone leaves a classroom, an office, or a seminar room, they can find themselves in another engaging space. In this way, circulation space can also be informal meeting space, lounge space, or dining space. This glue is as important as the discrete spaces that it holds together.

One of the major design challenges was achieving a different material expression for the faculty space and the student space. We decided to use variations in exterior and interior glazing to represent and distinguish between these two populations. With the student spaces, the aim was to maximize transparency. The offices required more privacy. After many iterations, we developed a gradient frit pattern for the glass that controls reflectivity, allowing for greater opacity or transparency according to the function of the room.

The circulation is such a striking element of the design, and it appears that it will be a quite active social space. Could you describe the flow of circulation in the building? Does the student or visitor move up from a porous ground floor? Are there degrees of publicness as one ascends the building?

45

Elizabeth Diller   The concept design was based on a vortex. The sweep of the building was envisioned as a fluid space in which circulation and communal space are one and the same. We always maintained the premise that classrooms are just one type of space for learning; the building's circulation— a connective tissue of informal meeting spaces—was another. It is a place for congregating, collaboration, and exchange. Formal design strategies emphasize this sense of contiguous space: the floors aren't just slab over slab over slab, like the way that the city is sliced up as discrete pieces of real estate. We pushed for porous spatial relationships vertically through the buildings.

Rendering of the western building of the Columbia Business School showing interior circulation and social spaces, 2015. Courtesy of Diller Scofidio + Renfro.

CR   In both the eastern and western buildings, there is one primary security line on the ground floor. The general public is not usually allowed past that security line, although there are exceptions. For the eastern building, for instance, we designed a space called the Forum, which is a 350-seat auditorium that opens to the public for events. Past the security line in each building, students, faculty, and staff can take one of two circulation paths. In the eastern building, students and administrators share these paths. The western building has two circulation paths that wind all the way to the top: one for faculty and one for students. It's like a double helix. At each level, there are shared social spaces for people to move between paths. It's a strategy that maintains some privacy while choreographing key moments of interaction. The two populations aren't isolated—they're intertwined.

ED   It was a process of realizing a concept with certain pragmatic and given guidelines. The first step was figuring out how the space of learning for a business school is different from that of other disciplines. At an early conversation with trustees and the leadership at Columbia, there was a suggestion to do away with classrooms altogether—to create one big café of sorts for people to drink and engage in both social and intellectual exchange. While that was clearly an exaggeration, it was also a powerful directive—the new business school needed to be a place where learning could happen informally, anywhere.

CR   Unprogrammed spaces in the buildings range considerably: from staircases with lounging cushions to seating areas with moveable furniture to learning environments with fixed tables and chairs. Even with the classrooms—the most recognizable of these spaces—we tried to reimagine and decontextualize the traditional setup by integrating new projection technology, optimizing natural light, and maximizing visibility with adjacent social spaces. Together, these spaces reflect a contemporary educational paradigm of communicating and learning together. And—most importantly—we ensured that there's always food involved.

ED   You can't think without food.

47

"Community" is a word frequently raised in regard to the Manhattanville campus, both by the university and by Renzo Piano. How did notions of public space and the community enter your thinking during the design process?

C R   From the very beginning, we knew that we wanted the buildings to have a meaningful interface with the neighborhood. The master plan guidelines required integrating elements independent of the project's academic function, like retail space and a public green that serves as a park for the neighborhood. In each of our architecture projects, our studio has always strived to blur the boundary between public and private space. We were excited to have this as a starting point for the design and pushed some of these concepts even further: we created a street-level café, for instance, that can be shared by students and visitors alike, and we opened certain parts of the building to the public, such as the small business incubator in the eastern building. The incubator is geared toward local businesses—it's a flexible space meant to facilitate start-up efforts for promising projects that have yet to become profitable enough to survive. The space could be used to develop an idea or product, or to actually sell something. It's close to the ground floor so that it can be visually accessible to the neighborhood.

The Forum and the Commons, Columbia Business School.
Courtesy of Diller Scofidio + Renfro.

I am also curious about the interaction between the business school and the other schools in the campus. Learning seems to function here differently than in the Mind Brain Behavior Institute, where one needs secure labs, or in the Lenfest Center, which houses performance spaces. How did you see this building fitting in with the ecology of the campus and the interdisciplinary learning it aims to facilitate?

E D   Renzo Piano conceived of an "urban layer" that would run through the entire Manhattanville campus. Each of the buildings on campus has a tall ground floor space that is independent of its respective discipline. This accessible space fuses all of the elements of the campus together. In our design for the business school, the urban layer is highly transparent and meant to encourage social activity. The Forum to the east and the Commons to the west will be open to the public. And between the two buildings, there will be a green quad—the Square—that not only adds an element of cohesion to the campus, but also provides accessible green space for the surrounding community.

CR   Students and faculty at the business school engage with a fascinating range of problem solving—from technology to art to nonprofits to banking. With the business school, we envisioned the public ground layer—and in particular the Square—as a place that brings everyone together to exchange ideas. There's a history at Columbia of the public green operating in this way: on the Morningside Heights campus, the quad is the heart of the school's social life. People hang out there year round, even in the snow. We wanted to bring that to this campus, too. Having the business school—with all its cross-disciplinary endeavors—as an anchor for that public green seems especially fitting.

It is true that the quad on the Columbia campus is well used by students, and also nonstudents at times, but how is the school conceived of differently than those on the Beaux Arts campus at Morningside?

ED   It's very different. Unlike Morningside, the Manhattanville campus has no surrounding walls and is connected with the urban fabric of the neighborhood. The campus is an extension of the city, and in our building design we tried to actively engage with the public openness of the site.

In early conversations about the project, one of our first questions was "How do you build a campus all at once?" It's a real challenge. The prospect of opening yet another campus with a massive master plan gave us pause. But the strength of the Manhattanville plan lies in its strategy of hiring different architects for different buildings. If this was the vision of one architect, it would be pretty repetitive—all one voice.

One striking thing in the renderings is how legible learning is from outside the building.

ED   Right. The building appears to be sliced in section: classrooms, meeting spaces, the auditorium, and circulation paths are right up against the walls. We wanted each building to make its learning spaces visible to the other building and to the public.

The Forum and the Commons, Columbia Business School. Images courtesy of Diller Scofidio + Renfro.

And the two buildings, was that part of the master plan, or was that a decision on your part?

ED It was the business school's decision, given the massive area required and the desire to have light throughout. From the start, this was a central challenge: how to create one school in two parts. We explored many types of relations of two: would the buildings be a pair? Or twins? Are they a theme and variation? Are they like Laurel and Hardy or Abbott and Costello—tall and skinny next to short and portly—or more like Fred and Ginger? In the final design, the proportions of each building are a bit different, but they're related, like siblings who share the DNA of their parents.

There is a visual communication between the two buildings. Distance allows you to see exactly how learning is being played out.

ED It was important for the two buildings to congeal into a mini campus across the Square, which in turn acts to cohere the larger campus.

1964

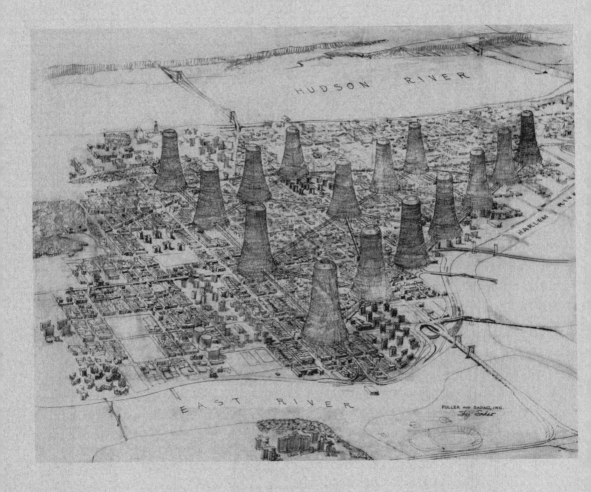

"A Skyrise for Harlem," Buckminister Fuller, Shoji Sadao, June Jordan, from 1965 issue of *Esquire*. Courtesy of the Estate of Buckminister R. Fuller.

Skyrise for Harlem

Towering above much of Harlem, the silo-like living cones of Skyrise for Harlem—a collaborative vision of June Jordan and Buckminster Fuller—were to rise in an array that spanned from the East River to the Hudson. Its westernmost edifices on the border of Manhattanville, enclosing block-sized extents of 125th Street, portions of public housing projects, and the many tenement buildings condemned as derelict in the neighborhood. This paper project was intended to challenge the prevailing logics of slum clearance and eminent domain and instead to offer a vision of urban revitalization that would not dislocate residents and raze homes but rather would provide a structure directly above houses in disrepair into which tenants could move. Skyrise created new avenues and thoroughfares elevated on suspension bridges and beneath its cylindrical supports, offering dynamic mobility. Ramps ran through the towers' interior cores, connecting workshops, grocery stores, parking, and even a family court. Parks and recreation areas distributed within its hundred-floor structures, carved green space out of sky. On the ground level, existing buildings would be razed after tenants had moved above, clearing space for a network of arterial parkland between the rivers. The tower bases produced curvilinear streets, disrupting the grid, with its trafficked corners and alleyways. Devices like heat-capturing lenses and rooftop rain-harvesting umbrellas would even distribute resources back into the city grid.

Jordan was an urban planner and a poet fiercely engaged with issues of environmental justice, urban politics, and race. She saw Skyrise as an opportunity to shape new possibilities for people living in Harlem, possibilities that—through design—cultivated community, elevated black culture in the public sphere, and offered remediation to the environmental burdens disproportionately shouldered by the urban poor. Her prescient thinking foreshadows the conversations about environmental justice the rezoning of Manhattanville raised decades later as residents spoke out about the effects of the MTA bus depot on 132nd Street and Broadway. "A half century of despair requires exorcism," she wrote in a 1965 *Esquire* article on the project. "The city is a model of design by accident, of construction in response to critical demand, high-level payoffs, and tax expediencies."[1]

In the months following the 1964 Harlem riots, Jordan, disappointed that environmental and urban design was not among the many remedies proposed to stem future violence, approached Buckminster Fuller, writing him to ask what could be done for Harlem. Architecture, she believed, was a powerful shaper of lived experience and what Harlem needed was "a radical reconstruction rather than a mere improvement into the middle-class physical chaos prized by the rest of the city." Skyrise for Harlem was their answer. Designed to be built in three years at low cost, the towers included a basic infrastructure of furniture, utilities, and parking—and were to be assembled by helicopter. Jordan hoped the project would "demonstrate the rational feasibility of beautiful and low-cost shelter integral to a comprehensively conceived new community for human beings."[2]

Jordan's sense of justice and accountability for Harlem and its residents, along with her expertise in urban planning and concern for environmental issues, was matched by Fuller's preoccupation with the problems (and possibilities) facing human settlements and ecologies. Their collaboration brought many of the design ideas Fuller had articulated in projects like the Dome over Manhattan and the 4D Towers—air purification, prefabrication, and central supportive masts, to name a few—into a specific, contingent, and urgent urban condition.

1
June Jordan, "Instant Slum Clearance," *Esquire*, vol. 63, no. 4 (April 1965): 111.

2
June Jordan quoted in Cheryl Fish, "Place, Emotion, and Environmental Justice in Harlem," *Discourse* (2007): 340.

A CAMPUS FOR TWENTY-FIRST CENTURY ARCHITECTURE

A Conversation with Robert Kasdin and Amale Andraos

In the following, Amale Andraos, Dean of Columbia University's Graduate School of Architecture, Planning, and Preservation speaks with the University's former Senior Executive Vice President Robert Kasdin about the changing nature of the campus in the twenty-first century and how Columbia worked with the New York City Planning Commission to rezone Manhattanville and make the campus possible.

Amale Andraos   I want to start with a question about the plan of the new campus. Between Renzo Piano Building Workshop, responsible for the architectural design; Skidmore, Owings & Merrill, who worked on the master plan; and the university team involved in the project, who made the decision to keep the city grid open as part of the campus layout?

Robert Kasdin   A decision was made pretty quickly that Columbia did not want to shut the streets that led from Broadway to the riverfront. There were really a number of reasons why. If you read Robert Caro's book on Robert Moses, Caro writes about how Moses deliberately did not continue the ribbon of parks up the West Side through and past 125th Street because Harlem was simply not a concern of his. For years the community has been trying to build park space on the waterfront. It seemed not only politically unwise but fundamentally wrong to block the community's access to this waterfront park they had waited so long for by shutting streets. So part of it was a sincere sensitivity to the surrounding community.

There was also a sense that unlike our beautiful early twentieth century campus, we should build a campus that was part of the city and part of the world. The Morningside Heights campus really is one of the finest examples of a certain attitude toward a campus: one with inner courtyards and green space, but one that is walled in and closed off from the outside world. Almost a hundred years later, we really wanted a campus that was integrated into the broader world, which is how our academic mission was being articulated and which represents our understanding of what it means to be Columbia University *in* the city of New York.

AA   It's interesting that you explain the plan as not just the image of the university and its current needs but also of what the university is becoming, what it will be in the future. University President Lee Bollinger often talks about that. It does feel like universities are changing and disciplines are being recast. It's like shedding an old skin and getting a new one where parts are slightly different. Is there a sense, or was there a sense, that the academic environment in Manhattanville would be different than in Morningside, both in terms of the disciplines and in terms of how people come together? Or was the campus project simply about space?

55

R K   I think there was a real commitment to try *not* to bind Columbia's future leadership to a particular vision of academic needs. What we instead hope for at Columbia is that when faculty identify a compelling line of intellectual inquiry and the university is able to bring funding to it, they have great space to pursue those academic needs.

As we moved through the city's approval process, we were pressed to identify the specific use of every potential building site, and I think that doing that would have been the wrong approach. So instead we have deliberately identified types of building use: Broadway is a big broad avenue that could support the blockiness of lab buildings, so we said we would be happy to use those as lab buildings or, depending on the site, academic buildings, which means primarily classrooms. But we didn't try to tie our successors to a particular vision of academic mission.

A A   That's quite interesting. I just had lunch with Tom Jessell and Richard Axel, whose labs will go into the new Mind Brain Behavior Institute. Specifically, we were discussing the ground floor: how to activate it and the possibility of finding the intersection between architecture and neuroscience as something that could be explored and made visible there. Once you have delimited a space, some of the questions that emerge around shaping it force the reorganization of the way we work.

The footprint of the plan itself is quite striking. I remember once you talked about how the footprints of the buildings are quite large. Was the intent of that to get the most out of the city, or was it an anticipated change, or could we use less of the space now that the master plan actually allows us to?

R K   The footprint of the massing envelopes of the buildings are stated in maximum terms rather than in required terms. And there is some limited ability to shift unused massing from site to site within a block. I think the city knew what it wouldn't permit but was not inclined, thankfully, to say anything in particular was required in terms of size and massing. For example, there are height restrictions. There are requirements with respect to walls: the plane of the walls needs to be broken after certain distances, and there can't be arcades. There are also all sorts of important aesthetic considerations and planning considerations built into the zoning text. But nothing requires us to build every site to the maximum available envelope.

A A   What was your biggest challenge, or were there moments when you thought this was just never going to happen? How long did the process take?

R K   We presented our plans to Community Board 9 for the first time on April 20, 2004. And we got approvals through ULURP (Uniform Land Use Review Procedure) from the city council in December of 2007. Considering the scale of the undertaking, it was actually quite fast.

Given the events of 1968, there was a lot of apprehension by some city and community leaders to get involved with Columbia University and Harlem. And I think that was the most significant obstacle. Could Columbia act as a trustworthy partner in doing the right thing, both for itself and for the surrounding community? There was also a sense that there would be some political risk associated with the project and that there are a lot of important things that the university could be doing that didn't have that political baggage.

Once New York City didn't receive the Olympics bid, the queue of proposals in front of the planning commission moved fairly quickly. I think that Deputy Mayor Dan Doctoroff, for example, always believed that the expansion of Columbia University and education in general was good for the economic development of the city. Mayor Bloomberg did as well. But there was that sense at a number of points that I had from other people that there was going to be a lot of political baggage and a lot of pain associated with Columbia's desire to expand in Harlem. The fact is, Harlem had changed and Columbia had changed, so when it came time to actually go through the approval process a lot of the concern was not borne by the experience.

A A   And will there be housing as part of the development?

R K   The university is required to build 830 apartments for faculty and graduate students on the Manhattanville campus. And there are certain sites that have been designated as either required or optional housing. Additionally there are over 300 housing units in what's referred to as 560 Riverside Drive. It's on the corner of Riverside Drive and 125th Street, brick buildings built I think in the late '60s, a couple of towers. And those will be opened to the north as they once were, and Columbia hopes these will generate foot traffic on 125th Street. The whole key is going to be making the area sufficiently dense.

57

A A   Yes, I think that's the big challenge, and that will take some time probably. But at the same time, it will allow the master plan to adjust itself, I think. Harvard is also expanding, but not in such close density and proximity. I can't think of another university that's managing to expand within a kind of city such as New York.

R K   There are a number of universities that have felt a need for more space. Columbia's effort to acquire, plan, and develop a large amount of space that is close to its current campus and use the world's great architects in doing so is unusual. This campus should be as important to twenty-first century architecture as the Morningside Heights campus was to early twentieth century architecture.

A A   It's true. Usually institutions would go for a more corporate sort of campus... What is one memory from the process that will stay with you?

R K   There are so many. There was the moment when I was standing in zero degree weather on 125th Street on the cell phone with Lee Bollinger really wondering whether it was ever going to happen. And then there was the moment when, for reasons I still don't understand, people who were in a position to allow us to move forward with ULURP all of a sudden opened the gates and said, "You're going now." These two moments bookend the process in terms of the sense of real puzzlement as to whether it would ever happen and real excitement that Columbia had finally reached the moment where it was going to have its opportunity to secure its physical future.

A A   As an architect, there's always at least one insecurity with one aspect of a project. In the meeting with Tom Jessell, for example, they were worried about the ground floor.

R K   I think ultimately our successors are going to need to relocate the bus terminal on the northernmost block. That is anticipated in the legal documents. We have secured the land under it, so once it's relocated, the land will be for Columbia to build on. But the hard work of finding a relocation site is not done. We have left that, for a host of very good reasons, to future generations of Columbia leadership, and it will be complicated because it will have implications for state, local, and federal law. And no one is anxious to have a bus terminal relocated to their neighborhood.

A A   With any luck, technology
will change.

R K   Yes. Probably faster than we think.

A A   How big was the team
working on the project?

R K   Well, there are different phases of the team.
In the pre-ULURP phase, we had our ULURP
consultants, and we had lawyers, and we had
Marilyn Taylor and Renzo Piano and RPBW. And it was
a lot of preparation. The preparation of the environmental
impact statement was all consuming for about two years.
I think once we got the requisite approvals, the nature
of the team shifted, and the ultimate users of the Jerome
L. Greene Science Center, for example—Richard Axel
and Eric Kandel and Tom Jessell and Charles Zucker—
became extremely important in designing a building
that would satisfy their research needs. Lawyers became
less pressing.
      The size of the team shifted over time. And I
think that the team within Columbia really changed. We
drew on extraordinary talents of people who work at
Columbia throughout the process, many of whom worked
24-7. I would get emails at three in the morning on
Saturday morning from Columbia employees working
on the project. And many of their names won't be recorded
anywhere in Manhattanville, but it was the result of their
amazing efforts that this all came to fruition.

1967

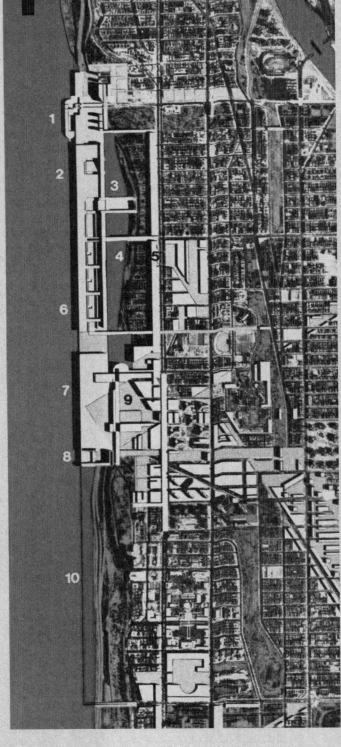

37

The Princeton team's site plan, Peter Eisenman and Michael Graves with G. Daniel Perry, Stephen Levine, Jay Turnbull, Thomas C. Pritchard, and Russell Swanson, as illustrated in *The New City* exhibition catalogue, 1967.

The New City: Architecture and Urban Renewal

The Museum of Modern Art's 1967 exhibition *The New City: Architecture and Urban Renewal* addressed four themes deemed urgent for New York City: "modification of the existing grid plan; housing without relocation; waterfront renewal; and new land."[1] According to Arthur Drexler, who organized the show at the suggestion of Peter Eisenman, these were the issues most vexing to urban planning and that contributed to social problems besetting the city in the late 1960s. By 1967, urban renewal had proven itself synonymous with the class and race discrimination latent in policies of slum clearance and eminent domain—policies that had displaced many New Yorkers in the preceding decades to make room for broader boulevards, civic spaces, and housing towers. The exhibition did not question whether the ends achieved by these policies were good or bad, but rather asked how to distribute civic investment equitably and realize these policy goals possible (new homes! public spaces! light and air!) without uprooting residents. So MoMA looked north, proposing a swath of Harlem—bounded by 96th Street to the south, 155th to the north, the Hudson to the west, and stretching east to encompass Wards and Randalls Islands and the South Bronx waterfront—for intervention.

The exhibition isolated four sites, corresponding to each of the curatorial themes, and assigned them to design teams from Cornell, Columbia, MIT, and Princeton. Princeton's contingent, led by Eisenman and Michael Graves, was provided with a stretch of Hudson-fronting land spanning from 125th to 155th Streets between Twelfth Avenue and the water. They were asked, "How can we make the waterfront both visible and useful, giving it an architectural weight that would relate it to major cross-town streets and lead to the development of new kinds of neighborhood and institutional centers?"[2] Their plan intended to increase accessibility to the waterfront by developing crosstown transportation arteries, linking existing parks and green spaces, and adding public amenities.

The architects suggested mass transit facilities be built along the 125th Street thoroughfare to connect to subway and commuter rail and that the street terminate in a large public plaza. Behind this plaza, a series of megastructures would line the river's edge. The proposed conference center, hotel, offices, stadium, and even aquarium were integrated into some of the neighborhood's existing fabric—the viaduct, the elevated subway, the wastewater treatment plant on 145th Street, to name a few. But gone were the meat market, the auto repair shops, and the printing facilities that gave the area economic vitality. As Richard Hatch, direc-

tor of the Architects' Renewal Committee in Harlem, wrote in an *Architectural Forum review*, "Blue collar employment opportunities are daily becoming rarer in New York City—with disastrous consequences. Yet the architects have replaced these 'noxious' uses with polite laboratories and research facilities, i.e. with jobs for other people."[3]

Hatch assailed the project for more than its economic classism: the scheme turned its back to the water and ignored existing uses and traffic; most significantly, it refused to sufficiently reimagine what West Harlem could look like, or could be. "The projects tend to treat Harlem as if it were simply an ugly place, a blemish to be repaired by cosmetic surgery," he wrote. By 1967, the New York City Housing Authority's modest coffers were quickly being depleted. Urban renewal that banked on research facilities and conference centers would effect little change to the material conditions of Manhattanville residents—concerns raised fifty years later when "polite laboratories" were again proposed for the site.

1
Arthur Drexler, ed., *The New City: Architecture and Urban Renewal* (New York: Museum of Modern Art, 1967), 23.

2
Drexler, *New City*, 22.

3
Richard Hatch, "The Museum of Modern Art Discovers Harlem," *Architectural Forum* 126 (March 1967): 38–47.

ARCHITECTURE AND ANALOGY
A Conversation with Thomas M. Jessell and Laura Kurgan

Thomas M. Jessell, Director of the Mortimer B. Zuckerman Mind Brain Behavior Institute, talks with Laura Kurgan, Director of the Center for Spatial Research, about the process of visualizing data, and how representations of data inform our perceptions of systems—be they cities or brains. The Center for Spatial Research is currently working with the Mind Brain Behavior Institute on *The Synapse*, an installation in the Jerome L. Greene Science Center that will communicate activity occurring in the labs to the public through dynamic display.

Laura Kurgan   I'd like to talk with you about how the visualization of data— something the disciplines of architecture and neuroscience share—actually informs and changes one's perception of space, be it of the city, of a building, or of the brain. I follow with interest developments in the new science of the brain, particularly the two different models of the brain: the functional model, where things are actually happening in the brain, and the network model, which tries to make sense of the complexity of information that is being transmitted in the brain. If an architecture student were to look at those two models and say, "These ideas might have an implication on the future of the city," could you help him or her tease some of them out?

Thomas M. Jessell   The networked model of the brain deals with the science of very large numbers of repeated elements, a science that is found, really, everywhere. Such magnitude of repetition is present in the cosmosphere when you look at stars and galaxies. It is absolutely present in the brain, and it is found in urban contexts too—in the conurbations where many, many people are packed together. In Manhattan, there are eight million people. In the brain there are eighty-six billion neurons. There are equivalent numbers of stars in the known universe. The question is, how do you deal with those numbers?

What that means is that we need to have people who are used to thinking about computations at a massive scale. The statisticians and theorists, therefore, will have an integral role in the Mind Brain Behavior Institute, people like Larry Abbott, the theoretical physicist turned neurobiologist. At the Mind Brain Behavior Institute, we are engaging disciplines outside of neuroscience. When discussing the possibilities for the building, Lee Bollinger, a First Amendment legal expert, said he would love for issues of free will and testimony to be rehearsed here. Those are very difficult things to achieve at the moment because of the vast intellectual divide that has to be bridged between the sciences and humanities pedagogically, but once we get momentum, programs like that can and will develop.

63

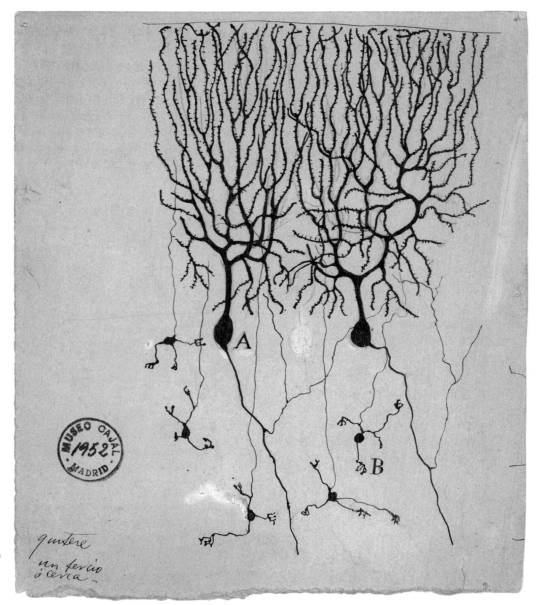

L K   Yes, it's clearly a question of scale, of different scale, and I appreciate the idea that what looks rather small, compared to a city, itself involves some huge numbers and a lot of calculations. And I hope you're right that this will be an opportunity to make the leap from the sciences to the humanities and back. But in a sense it's already happening, and has historical precedent. Just look at the aesthetics of the drawings of Santiago Ramón y Cajal, the father of modern neuroscience, and some of the mesmerizing images in the book *Portraits of the Mind*, by Columbia student Carl Schoonover. This is how brain science is communicated, and there's a lot of design in it. The technologies that produce these images are often built on the revolutionary techniques that change our ways of seeing and describing the living world.

T J   Because the brain has eighty-six billion neurons, or nerve cells, there is an element of repetition in it. In mammals, one could argue that no individual nerve cell is unique. Each one has siblings that are trying to do the same thing, because one nerve cell alone is not capable of commanding behavior. This repetition leaves open the ability for patterns to emerge where you look at many, many different neurons of the same type and you see morphologies that are individual to that class of neurons. So a seasoned anatomist can look at a class of neurons and tell you where that neuron is found in the brain, what it looks like, and, sometimes, what it does.

Neurons are simple and wonderful structures. They have a cell body that contains their genetic material. Then unlike, say, a liver cell, which is essentially spherical, neurons have elaborate projections that branch out to communicate with and receive information from other neurons, which are often far away. To do this they extend these branches, known as axons, and receive thousands of inputs from other neurons. We refer to them as branches because they look like trees, and in part they function like trees in terms of receiving input from different sources in the sensory world.

There are two types of neuroscientists, I think. There are those who have learned to think in a numerate world—the statisticians and former physicists. And then there are those who are very taken with pattern and form and get their inspiration from looking down microscopes at the imagery of neuronal communication. Ramón y Cajal was the most dramatic and renowned exponent of this form of inference. He could look through the microscope and resolve almost every aspect of functional neuroanatomy and neurobiology that existed. This form of neural science is very closely related, I think, to architectural thinking, where structure and pattern and form are so elemental. If you look at Renzo Piano's architecture, there is a biological elemental core. His Kansai Airport design resembles a lizard-like skeleton. And his more recent dome of the California Academy of Sciences in San Francisco evokes a virus capsid. Parallels between architectural and natural forms can be found everywhere.

L K   Those are the frozen forms of architecture, the ones that are actually structuring physical space. But there are other kinds of architecture that are built out of networks and invisible spaces, and these are often described through metaphors. We are addressing some of these metaphors in our project, *The Synapse*, which aims to address the more invisible and networked space of the Mind Brain Behavior Institute, especially in its most accessible public space. I want to bring up one metaphor that was in the press a lot when the Nobel Prize was awarded last year to a group of neuroscientists for their discovery of nerve cells for spatial navigation, "the brain's positioning system."

In the 1960s, the urban planner Kevin Lynch published *The Image of the City*. It offered a theory of urban navigation based on known markers in the city, according to which people would orient themselves. "Cognitive mapping" and "wayfinding" became the watchwords of Lynchian urbanism. Did those Nobel scientists—John O'Keefe, maybe—read Lynch? He seems to think about orientation and the city in a very similar way. How did this idea move from being a metaphor for urban orientation to an actual model of cognition?

T J   John is a New Yorker. He works in London now but was born and raised in the Bronx, so he regards himself as both a New Yorker and a Londoner combined. The idea that the hidden lives of cities have organismal reality is really true I think. And so you can look at a city and you can look at an organism and make parallels there in terms of arterial routes of communication.

What I had found somewhat inappropriate about that analogy is that it is slightly trivializing. John O'Keefe became famous for the discovery of place cells, not grid cells. He showed that there are regions of the brain that are aware of your environment. So in the hippocampus, if you record from a neuron, that neuron is active only when, for example, an animal is in a specific location—what that neuron does is integrate bits of spatial information from the structure of the room around it, and it uses this information to keep tabs on where an object is. The place cell, in essence, encodes the awareness of surroundings.

Grid cells came along thirty years after place cells and were discovered by Edvard and May-Britt Moser.

They were found in a region of cortex that is hard to access. Place cells were discovered in the early 1970s, whereas grid cells were first recorded in 2005. So there was a long gap between the discovery of place and grid cells.

Grid cells are similar to place cells except that instead of sampling one unique location, they monitor a hexagonal pattern of positional information. And as you move deeper from one surface of the region of the brain known as entorhinal cortex, the space in which that hexagonal pattern represents the world changes progressively, creating a scalar as well as positional map.

This hexagonal array of grid cell activities fills the brains of neurobiologists with all sorts of interesting questions: How do you achieve spatial scale invariance? What is the relationship between grid and place? Resolving these questions is hard because we are deep in the brain—the region that Vernon Mountcastle called "the big in between." The hippocampus is not a sensory system that can be understood when applying a simple sensory stimulus. It's, as Mountcastle stated, right in the middle. So the behavioral outputs that are measured are transformed by many, many synaptic inputs. Working in this middle ground and understanding what goes on in it is very difficult, so the grid cell was a great discovery. It is also intriguing as a romantic notion of position and the sense of place.

L K   Does that metaphor accurately capture how the institute will sit inside the building? There might not be such a comfortable one-to-one relationship between the three-dimensional space of the building and the research that occurs inside it.

T J   Yes. I think of the building as a living Rubik's Cube. It looks like a cube and has the same overall structure. It is intended to be three-dimensional—the interactions between one floor and the floor above or below are going to be just as relevant as the horizontal connections between these different quad-like structures. It's also a bit Rubikoid in the sense that it produces the same effect as the shifting of a Rubik's Cube: it creates the ability for everybody in the building to interact with one another.

1968

Drawing and photograph from the Architects'
Renewal Committee in Harlem and the West
Harlem Community Organization Inc. proposal
for the site of the Columbia University gym,
from *West Harlem Morningside: A Community
Proposal*, 1968.

Columbia University Gym Protests

In 1959, Columbia University began formulating plans for a new gymnasium for Columbia College students in Morningside Park, along the campus's eastern border. The plan would not get off the ground until the mid-1960s, by which time community groups in West Harlem, and the residents they represented, had developed significant opposition to the proposal because it would expropriate land that served the recreational needs of Harlem residents with few concessions to the community. Furthermore, renderings of high, unbroken walls conjured a language of fortification and separation. Despite these reservations, as well as opposition from many Columbia students and faculty members, construction of the gym began in February 1968—a year that would be remembered as a volatile one, marked by protest movements worldwide.

Harlem residents were provided a separate entrance on the eastern side of the park, down the hill from the university—an architectural decision that came to symbolize the class and race tensions between the university and its surrounding community. Lambasted as the "Jim Crow door," this separate entrance gave Harlemites access only to parts of the gym for limited hours of the day, demonstrating both the architects' and Columbia's segregation of facilities along racial lines, in what *New York Times* architecture critic Ada Louise Huxtable called, "a definitive demonstration of institutional failure to comprehend and react to the human and urban attitudes that surround it."[1] The protesters—organized by Students for a Democratic Society, the Student Afro-American Society, and neighborhood associations—rallying against the gym construction for much of the spring of '68, put it more directly. The construction of the gym was evidence of, "the university's racism and refusal to deal with the community."[2]

Ultimately, the protests (which had been disbanded in a cloud of tear gas and arrests) and local outcry were successful; construction on the gym halted by the fall. If on the one hand the gym proposal had unearthed the frustration and outrage latent in the community, the vacant construction site and coalition building generated different forms of architectural speculation for the neighborhood as well. Later that year, the Architects' Renewal Committee of Harlem (ARCH), headed by J. Max Bond—the future chairman of architecture at Columbia University's Graduate School of Architecture, Planning, and Preservation—along with the West Harlem Community Organization submitted a proposal for Morningside Park not only to address the massive hole Columbia had left in the ground, but also to provide the community services the gym proposal had failed to include: an amphitheater, a swimming pool and ice rink, a community center, a cycling and pedestrian connection to Central Park, better lighting, and maintenance.[3] As is obvious to anyone who goes to Morningside Park today, whose northern edge on 123rd Street abuts the southern border of Manhattanville, ARCH's plan did not come to pass. Dismissed by groups like the Friends of Central Park as "junk," Morningside Park was eventually returned to its previous, more pastoral, condition. While the scars of Columbia's ill-fated construction were balmed with grassy fields and duck ponds, the wounds inflicted on community relations remained, continuing to color university expansion proposals as callous land grabs up to the present.

1
Ada Louise Huxtable, "How Not to Build a Symbol," *New York Times*, March 24, 1968.

2
"Press Statement of Black Students in Hamilton Hall (Ray Brown)," *Columbia University Libraries Online Exhibitions*, http://exhibitions.cul.columbia.edu/exhibits/show/1968/item/5536.

3
Gail Robinson, "Community Reveals Plans for Park," *Columbia University Spectator*, October 2, 1972.

A SMALL MACHINE
An Interview with Carol Becker

Carol Becker, Dean of Columbia University School of the Arts, along with faculty, staff, and the Director and Chief Curator of the Miriam and Ira D. Wallach Art Gallery, Deborah Cullen, collaborated with the Renzo Piano Building Workshop to envision a state-of-the-art performance, screening, exhibition, and events facility for the university: the Lenfest Center for the Arts. In the following interview with editor Caitlin Blanchfield, Becker discusses the spatial needs of a twenty-first century venue building and the critical research underway in the arts.

Renzo Piano describes the Manhattanville campus as a space that is public and transparent—a beacon of openness. But I imagine performing arts and arts programs have different requirements for how to bring those concepts in without necessarily using the same architectural metaphors of glass or open plans. What was your vision for the Lenfest Center, and what are the building's programmatic needs? How was that reconciled within a building that is designed in the same architectural language as a larger campus?

Carol Becker   Renzo Piano's original concept for the building was a glass cube. He called it "the Lantern," and we called it the Lantern for a long time, until Gerry and Marguerite Lenfest made the primary gift to the building. Then it became the Lenfest Center for the Arts.

The Lenfest Center was always going to be a venue building— it is too small for visual arts production, for example, and we have Prentis Hall across the street for that purpose, with some space for film and other programs. We also have production space in Nash Hall. Because it was to be a multipurpose venue, a glass cube surely would never have worked for a film-screening room or a flexible performance space. When it became clear that the Wallach Art Gallery also was coming into the building, the concept had to be rethought. You really can't put an art gallery in a glass cube.

The top floor is an open space that can be reconfigured for exhibitions, symposia, readings, or events. Because of the size of the floor plate, all of these different functions had to be stacked, which is also complicated. We had to pay a great deal of attention to how the building actually would function. Considering the possibility that all floors might be activated at the same time, a lot of thought has gone into how to prevent sound from leaking between floors.

Through much close discussion and negotiation, we were able to come to a mutual understanding of what the building would be. In Renzo Piano's grand scheme for the campus, the Lenfest Center is a pivotal node holding different architectural elements together. When you walk onto the new campus, at least on the 125th Street side, you'll walk onto the small square or piazza and come right up to our building—it is a linchpin for the other buildings to come.

71

What were the design decisions that facilitated all this stacked functioning in such a tight space?

C B It's small, and in such a situation you can't waste an inch. You have to maximize the functionality. And because each floor houses potentially different users, we had to make the building work well as one vertical entity. The building has to function like a small machine, which is something we talked about a lot with Renzo Piano. It's like the Centre Pompidou for him in some ways because it too is an experimental art space, albeit quite small.

But it's not the Isabella Stewart Gardner Museum. It's not the Art Institute of Chicago. It was never going to be a large building. The Lenfest Center is not a museum-scale building. It houses the Wallach Art Gallery, which needs museum-quality lighting and museum-quality facilities so that it can hold wonderful exhibitions and accommodate borrowed artwork. But it is a building that has to work for many distinct functions. Every floor has specific needs. That was the hard part: communicating and negotiating those needs, in practical and aesthetic terms. Conversations around design centered on questions like, "Who is going to use it? What do we want it to do? What do we want it to look like?"

Every chair for the Katharina Otto-Bernstein Screening Room and flexible performance space, for example, has been a conversation in terms of functionality, comfort, and design. Should it have arms? What should the color be so it doesn't reflect light? Should there be cup holders for water? Do we want people to bring in water or not? Will they bring it in anyway, and so, anticipating this, should we have cup holders? I mean, literally everything has been a conversation between faculty, staff, and Renzo Piano's team.

I was struck by the idea in your book, *Thinking in Place*, that architecture should encourage us to take risks, change the culture of existing tastes, but engage us in serious types of play. Do you think that play as a form of experimentation is present in this architecture?

C B I'll answer with an analogy that might sound odd. Whenever we, at the School of the Arts, want to redo our logo, it becomes a huge event. Art schools are notoriously difficult clients to please because people have such strong ideas about visuals. But often designers come in with really offbeat concepts of what our logo should look like. And I always say, "You know, we really don't need a funky logo. Actually what we need is a classical logo that looks contemporary." *We* are the wild part, so in terms of how we think about the Lenfest Center, the building is the container for experimentation, play, and wildness. What we needed was a very elegant machine.

72

We didn't need a building to look like an art piece because it's going to be full of art pieces—and Renzo Piano understands this very well. The museums he has built are classical contemporary. For us to play in the space, the building has to disappear. It cannot compete. The industrial look is inspiring to artists. It has a rawness to it—a building waiting to be utilized.

To me, it is an elegant building. It's cool for the kind of hot content it will contain. If it were competing with the work by being too jazzy, that would be problematic. Also, it has to work in conjunction with the Jerome L. Greene Science Center next door. In some parts of the Lenfest Center, you can almost touch the neuroscience building—it is that close. So it's not a building standing entirely on its own. It has to work in context.

And how has the school connected to the area or to the surrounding community?

CB We're going to be on 125th Street with a lot of other very important cultural institutions that are also evolving—for example, the Studio Museum in Harlem is going through an expansion with David Adjaye. Many things are shifting in the adjacent neighborhoods right now.

We have partnered with many organizations in Harlem for some time. Our students have been teaching writing through the Columbia Artist/Teachers program, for example. But now we are actually coming into the neighborhood ourselves, and because the campus will have no gates, its urban layer will feel very accessible. We'll be another cultural entity in the neighborhood. We're going to have a cinematheque on the weekends when the space is not being used for classes. We are going to have readings, exhibitions, and performances. I think many people on the West Side are going to want to come see what we are doing and, hopefully, we'll be working in partnership with many other organizations and inviting their audiences into our space as well.

Construction of the Wallach Art Gallery. Courtesy of the Manhattanville Development Group.

Construction of flexible performance space in the Lenfest Center. Courtesy of the Manhattanville Development Group.

How can the building facilitate these interactions between students and the community, and between disciplines in the university?

C B   I'll give you an example. Let's say the MFA Visual Arts Thesis Show is up in the Wallach Art Gallery and using the two top floors. The gallery dealers and art world people will come. They always do. They have come to Long Island City, where the Thesis Show has been exhibited for the past eight years, and they have picked up artists for their galleries and exhibitions. But who doesn't come? Students from other disciplines at Columbia, undergraduates, faculty from other disciplines, cultural leaders from the adjacent neighborhoods, other college communities, and high school students tend not to attend. We can change all this just by being closer to Columbia and closer to Harlem and the West Side. So if we invite people in and we schedule artist talks and we have artists walking people through the galleries, for example, we will be bringing whole new constituencies into our art-making process. That's something that wouldn't have happened before. The building is designed for public interaction, and it is in a neighborhood with great art traditions and many interested people. Also, the Wallach Art Gallery can now control its hours of operation. We can make our own exhibitions more pedagogical to be sure. The links between process and finished product will be more accessible, which is what art schools are able to do.

Commercial galleries present work: "Here's the product. This is the price." But we're about how artists get from here to there. How do artists even get in the mind-set to move from here to there? It helps to hear artists talk about the work; otherwise, art can be very mystifying. People always ask: "What made you think to do that?" When artists talk about their work, there is a logic to how they navigated from concept to actualization. And it's very pedagogical to hear them explain it.

So we can put art programming together in a way that's never been possible before, and Columbia can say, "The arts are a vital part of what Columbia does as a research institution. The university has a huge arts research component happening every day." We've never been able to show that to the campus, let alone to the city.

And how would you say that the arts
are research-based?

CB The arts create new
knowledge. Every time
someone experiments
using new materials, pushing visual boundaries, using
new technologies, taking ideas and giving them form, it is
research—in the arenas of storytelling, visual and sound
acuity, and so forth.

How do you communicate complicated ideas in
writing? How do you write the twenty-first century memoir
about being a diasporic Syrian? How do you produce a play
about complex issues of race and class in America? How do
you make a film that communicates what is going on now in
conflict zones or post-conflict zones around the world? How
do you write plays or make art about being a first-generation
immigrant from Kenya? Or tell the story of growing up
gay in Wyoming? Or create an interactive installation or
sound piece about climate change? This is the work that
is currently being done in our MFA and MA programs. Art
really is an idea given form. So what are those ideas asking
to be represented, and what are the forms that can contain
them? Finding forms to represent the relationship of the
individual to the collective at this time in history creates
new knowledge. It is the research and experimentation the
School engages in every day. Now we will have a building that
will allow us to invite the public into that process.

Construction of the Wallach Art Gallery.
Courtesy of the Manhattanville Development Group.

75

The Construction of Manhattanville: June 2016
Photographs by Tom Harris

The Construction of Manhattanville: June 2016 documents the many views of the Manhattanville neighborhood around the time of this book's publication. As construction of the Jerome L. Greene Science Center and the Lenfest Center near completion, and as other parts of the site continue to be developed, Columbia's new campus appears at times as a prominent flurry of activity, and at other times barely visible among the neighborhood's housing towers, trestles, viaduct, and daily life.

1989

FOCUS

A community divides over Harlem on the Hudson

By Alex Roth

The strip of 12th Avenue from 125th to 133rd Street is run-down and empty save the meat packaging and storage companies scattered on both sides of the street.

One block to the west is Marginal Street, a desolate roadway that runs along the bank of the Hudson River and that forms the western border of a poor, mostly black and Hispanic Lower West Harlem community.

The Harlem Urban Development Corporation, a Harlem-based public agency, wants to turn this area into a $400 million entertainment, business and cultural center as large and fancy as the Southstreet Seaport. The purpose of the project, the agency says, would be to reestablish Harlem as the world capital of black and Latino culture and to revitalize a community where almost 50 percent of the households earn less than $12,500 a year.

In August a private consultant firm was given $300,000 to study the feasibility of "Harlem on the Hudson," as the development would be called. The study will take nine months, and it could take another year or more to get all the state and city approval needed for a project this size. But if it's ever built, Harlem on the Hudson will be the biggest development West Harlem has ever seen.

The question of whether it should be built has the Harlem community divided. Many local politicians, religious and business leaders and others fiercely support the plan, but other community leaders and urban experts say the project is a wild fantasy that will displace

> *It's good for our children to see doctors and lawyers. Right now our children don't see anyone but crack dealers.*
> —HCCI President Preston Washington

residents, remove good jobs, and do the community more economic harm than good. The controversy pits the two sides in a battle that raises basic questions about what's best for the downtrodden area.

"There are a lot of real issues involved with this project," says Coy LaSister, director of markets for New York City's Department of Ports and Trade and a member of the Harlem on the Hudson Task Force. "There are a lot of critical issues that have to be addressed."

A $35,000 HUDC public relations campaign advertises Harlem on the Hudson as "a new leisure capital." The strip of land that houses the meat markets would be turned into a glitzy "Street of Sound" lined with ethnic restaurants and night clubs for jazz, reggae, and Latino music. A giant cultural arts center showcasing the talents of black and Latino artists would extend over the Hudson River on a huge floating complex. The plan also calls for a large hotel, a marina, and industrial space for high-tech corporations.

The agency promises about 1800 units of housing by the pier—about 30 percent low-income and the rest market-rate. Most, if not all, of the low-income housing would be reserved for artists and the elderly, according to the latest blueprint.

Financing will come from private as well as public sources. Last year, in fact, a group of real estate executives from Tokyo spent three days touring the neighborhood and studying the agency's development proposal.

The proposal's supporters—among them Congressman Charles Rangel and Assemblywoman Geraldine Daniels—say Harlem on the Hudson will give West Harlem the sort of spiritual and cultural vigor it hasn't seen since the first half of the century. What's more, they say, it will pump economic life into an area that gets more depressed every year.

"I've been a pastor here for 13 years," says Preston Washington of Harlem Churches for Community Improvement. "The community has just died. I've seen the destruction of two or three generations of black males. We need to have projects of a certain magnitude."

Proponents say Harlem on the Hudson

Top: Marginal Street, on the bank of the Hudson River, is now a barren runway (Photo by Olga Zvenyatsky). Right: An artist's rendition of the proposed "Street of Sound" (Courtesy HUDC).

would help bring the best in black and Latino culture to a community that has seen the arts slowly seep away over the decades. Today there are only two performing arts facilities in Harlem, the Apollo Theater and Aaron Davis Hall, HUDC officials point out. Washington and others say the development could help return Harlem to the days of Duke Ellington, Charlie Parker and Miles Davis.

HUDC officials and other proponents of the plan also say Harlem on the Hudson will make perfect use of the deteriorated pier area. A waterfront area that is now empty and unused could be turned into the central nervous sytem of the entire community, they say. "Our waterfront should be exploited the same way every community exploits its waterfront," says HUDC Chief Architect Rudy Dupuy.

More important, proponents say, Harlem on the Hudson will bring money and jobs to West Harlem, where by some estimates 30 percent of the population is unemployed. HUDC officials promise an influx of permanent blue- and white-collar jobs to West Harlem. "There will be managerial jobs, opportunities to own new businesses," says HUDC spokesman Rufus Rivers. Rivers says residents will be

SPECTATOR/ANDREW ROSENBLATT
Tom Demott and others from the West Harlem Coalition oppose Harlem on the Hudson. Others in community fiercely support it.

given job training to prepare them for back-office employment and other skilled labor.

Some supporters see other benefits to the middle-class influx. "It's good for our children to see doctors and lawyers," says Preston Washington of Harlem Churches for Community Improvement. "Right now our children don't see anyone but crack dealers."

But others in the community have serious reservations about the plan—and many ex-

perts familiar with the project are also skeptical. "HUDC wants a feather in its cap, and the best way to do it is by building a grand project," says Elliot Sclar, a professor of urban planning at Columbia who advises community boards in the city. "Anybody who wants to do an upscale project all of a sudden develops a keen interest in the poor."

The last place for a giant arts center and a glitzy night-club district is an area as blighted as West Harlem, critics say. And, they add, the $400 million that would be spent on the project is a total misuse of public funds that could be much better spent in the community.

Most opponents worry that Harlem on the Hudson will wind up being a high-profile tourist trap with no place for local residents. The new restaurants and shops will be geared to tourists, not to people who live in the area, they say. Critics also say most residents won't be suited for many of the new jobs that come to the pier area. Rather than training local residents, businesses will simply hire better-qualified people from outside the community, they say.

One of the biggest criticisms of the development is that the eleven meat markets lining 12th Avenue would have to be relocated to make room for the Street of Sound, meaning close to 300 relatively-high paying manufacturing jobs would leave the community.

HUDC officials say the markets would be moved either to Hunt's Point or Brooklyn. HUDC would have to get the approval from the meat market owners before the markets are moved. But LaSister says most of the owners are willing to move since the buildings the businesses would be moved to are much nicer than the ones they occupy now.

Says Zaharis Kalaitzis of the West Harlem Coalition, a local tenant organization: "People who were making working-class incomes [at the meat markets] will have to take

dishwashing jobs at $3.75 an hour."

Perhaps the largest danger—and the opponents' biggest fear—is that Harlem on the Hudson will open the community to the gentrification that is creeping up the west side of Manhattan. "The housing they're proposing is going to rise above the viaduct, with a view of the Hudson River," says Jean Flatow of West Harlem's Community Board 9. "You tell me that's not going to wind up luxury housing?" No one lives in the area HUDC wants to develop. But opponents worry about "secondary displacement." They say a project like Harlem on the Hudson would make land values skyrocket, forcing local storeowners' rents to rise. The stores would have to either raise their prices or leave for fancier stores. Either way, opponents say, the cost of living would rise beyond the means of local residents.

"[Secondary displacement] is already hap-

> *Anyone who wants to do an upscale project all of a sudden develops a keen interest in the poor.*
> —Professor of Urban Planning Elliot Sclar

pening by Columbia," says the West Harlem Coalition's Tom Demott. "The Upper West Side is the hottest property in the city. You can just see how the composition of the neighborhood is changing."

Experts familiar with Harlem on the Hudson admit revitalizing an area as depressed as West Harlem is no simple task. In an age and area when mixing a neighborhood's income can quickly lead to gentrification, building too much low-income housing can overburden local social services and deprive the community of any economic life. Many experts say it's sometimes impossible to reach a stable balance between gentrification and ghettoization.

Some experts, like Columbia Professor of Architectural Planning Rob Burlage, say a better approach to this sort of community development would be to promote a limited middle-class influx while using public money to develop a broad social services network in the community.

"You have to be very cautious in this type of situation," Burlage says. "You can't just use the trickle-down theory as a panacea."

In a rebuttal to HUDC's approach to local development, Community Board 9 this summer released a proposal suggesting that all 1,130 vacant city-owned housing units be developed by the city and made available to an income mix that mirrors the community's current income profile.

The plan also suggests taking all local va-

See Harlem, p. 12

"A Community Divides Over Harlem on the Hudson," from the *Columbia Daily Spectator*, November 13, 1989.

Harlem on the Hudson

The Harlem Urban Development Corporation (HUDC), founded in 1971 by Governor Nelson A. Rockefeller, aimed to combat what was seen as commercial and residential blight in Harlem. Intended to quell opposition to development in the area in the 1960s—and responding in particular to the 1969 protests against Rockefeller's state high-rise building on 125th Street and Seventh Avenue, today known as the Adam Clayton Powell Jr. State Office Building—the HUDC operated under community control. In many ways, Rockefeller intended it to act as a mediator between the state and the community. Harnessing power in the name of "the people," the organization sought to oppose outside, or "downtown," interests through its own community agendas.[1]

By the 1980s, after the Manhattanville meat-processing and wholesale distribution industries had been incentivized to move to Hunts Point in the Bronx, manufacturing and industry in the area dramatically declined—and with it the larger commercial workforce.[2] The HUDC initiated a series of planning studies, including the 1989 plan Harlem on the Hudson by the firm Abeles Phillips Preiss & Shapiro, in an attempt to revitalize the area, now characterized by the warehouses, garages, and parking lots scattered across it. Perhaps not unlike planners before him, HUDC chief architect Rudy Dupuy proclaimed, "Our waterfront should be exploited the same way every community exploits its waterfront."[3]

Due to the site's advantageous position along the Hudson River, Harlem on the Hudson proposed a waterfront promenade to function as the neighborhood's central nervous system. The plan also envisioned a 300-to-500-seat theater, restaurant cruise boat, live-work space for artists and artisans, a new consolidated meat market facility, and a series of commercial, retail, and cultural spaces. The Harlem on the Hudson Feasibility Study was eventually published in 1992; however, the project was never realized due to the area's poor real estate market in the 1990s, as well as insufficient funding and general lack of community consensus.

Perhaps equally important to this story was the ultimate failure of the HUDC. The corporation suffered criticism from the community; many believed it was an ineffective generator of economic growth and housing.[4] Some accused the HUDC of being a "patronage machine"—Harlem's gatekeeper for development fueled by the political ambitions of elected officials like Congressman Charles Rangel.[5] The corporation officially closed its doors in 1994, under allegations of corruption, malfeasance, and misappropriation of funds. That same year, Harlem waterfront was designated part of the Upper Manhattan Empowerment Zone—one of nine zones in effect during the Clinton administration—to revitalize the neighborhood through public funds and tax incentives.

1
Kimberley Johnson, "Community Development Corporations, Participation, and Accountability: The Harlem Urban Development Corporation and the Bedford-Stuyvesant Restoration Corporation," Annals of the American Academy of Political and Social Science 594 (2004): 109–124.

2
For statistics on the decline of Manhattanville's industry, see Maxine Griffith, "Manhattanville: A Personal History," in this volume, 96–107.

3
Alex Roth, "A Community Divides over Harlem on the Hudson," Columbia Daily Spectator, November 13, 1989.

4
Brett Pulley, "End of Urban Agency Draws Fears of Neglect," New York Times, March 30, 1995.

5
Johnson, "Community Development Corporations," 121; Derek S. Hyra, The New Urban Renewal: The Economic Transformation of Harlem and Bronzeville (Chicago: University of Chicago Press, 2008).

MANHATTANVILLE: A PERSONAL HISTORY

MAXINE GRIFFITH

My father, McCleod Isaiah Griffith, immigrated to the United States from the island of Barbados in the British West Indies. He came via a circuitous route, first traveling to Haiti, where he lived for several years, then moving on to Cuba, where he learned Spanish by pointing at people and objects with a long stick. He planned to stop in the United States only for a few weeks to visit his older brother and to see the skyscrapers. McCleod, whom everyone called Mac, was on his way to Paris. He had been told, by a lovely young woman that Paris was a great place for a black man.

My uncle Edwin, much older than my father, had come to America years before. With money he made working in the mud helping to build the Panama Canal, he bought property in Brooklyn and lived comfortably, reminiscing about the "old country" with his Jamaican, Barbadian, and Trinidadian neighbors and tenants. He told his brother Mac that he should stay in New York for a while and make a little more money before continuing on to Europe. Although my father, a skilled carpenter and cabinetmaker, had done well in Cuba, he decided that his older brother was right. There was a housing boom in the borough of Queens—he would stay for a few months, maybe a year, and enter the French capital as a man of substance. He wrote to the young woman, maid to a prominent French family, who had told him of the wonders of Paris and said that he would see her in a year. But many years later, as a man in his late fifties living in Harlem, he married my mother, Madye Elizabeth Gray in a City Hall ceremony. I was born in Harlem Hospital.

My father loved New York. He was already a baseball enthusiast and quickly became a fan of hamburgers and fried chicken and apple pie from the automat. But sometimes he would yearn for the foods of his youth: cou-cou and flying fish, codfish cake, rice and peas, and curry goat. When the desire for goat descended, he would set off to Harlem from Brooklyn, where we had moved. Dressed in his Saturday corduroy pants and plaid work shirt, and with his small daughter in hand, he'd take the A train and then walk what seemed like a very long way to Twelfth Avenue under the viaduct to the meat market in Manhattanville—a loud, lively, colorful, and polyglot place.

Manhattanville sits in a valley known as Moertje David's Vly during Dutch colonization, or the Hollow Way during the American

96

1 Eric K. Washington, *Manhattanville: Old Heart of West Harlem* (Charleston, SC: Arcadia Publishing, 2002), 7. See also "Honoring Manhattanville's History," http://manhattanville.columbia.edu/honoring-manhattanvilles-history.

2 Mary Stockwell, "Battle of Harlem Heights," *The Digital Encyclopedia of George Washington*, http://www.mountvernon.org/digital-encyclopedia/article/battle-of-harlem-heights. See also Mark Mayo Boatner, *Cassell's Biographical Dictionary of the American War of Independence, 1763–1783* (London: Cassell, 1966).

3 Washington, *Manhattanville*, 73.

4 Washington, *Manhattanville*, 7.

5 Susan S. Lukesh, "Jacob Schieffelin (1757–1835)," *Immigrant Entrepreneurship: German-American Business Biographies*, http://immigrantentrepreneurship.org/entry.php?rec=124.

Revolution. This was where the main action of the Battle of Harlem Heights began.[1] In 1776 "the Continental Army had retreated to the northern end of Manhattan following its humiliating loss at the Battle of Long Island."[2] The army of about 1,800 men was led by General George Washington. Although this anecdote may be apocryphal, we were told that British troops made a tactical error by having their light infantry buglers sound a fox-hunting call called "gone away" while in pursuit of the then-retreating "Americans." This was intended to taunt Washington, himself a keen fox hunter—"gone away" means that a fox is in full flight from the hounds on its trail. The Continentals, infuriated by this insult, determined to stay and hold their ground. The successful Battle of Harlem Heights restored public confidence in the American troops and lifted the spirits of the Continental Army.[3]

While the battle made the area well known, it wasn't until 1806 that the village of Manhattanville was formally established around the crossroads of Bloomingdale Road and Manhattan Street, now known as Broadway and 125th Street.[4] The neighborhood stretched roughly from 122nd north to 135th Street, west to the water, and east up its slope to what is now Adam Clayton Powell Jr. Boulevard.

Jacob Schieffelin (born August 24, 1757), the Philadelphia-born son of a German immigrant, helped to lay out a grid of streets in the hollow between the hills of Morningside Heights to the south and Washington Heights to the north. Schieffelin, a wealthy merchant, worked with other members of the commercial class, many of whom were Quakers, to promote the area as a center of trade and commerce. At the time, the village would have been eight miles north of what was New York City and west of the incorporated Village of Haarlem. Schieffelin purchased and sold many tracts of land in the area, with the intention to establish a planned community in this underdeveloped portion of upper Manhattan. His plan included buying residential and businesses properties, as well as introducing industry, and even educational and religious institutions, to the neighborhood.[5] In 1806 the village of Manhattanville was established with a grid that resisted the Cartesian coordinates of much of the island to follow the natural topography of the area, embracing its existing harbor, pastures, and farms. Stables, warehouses, icehouses, and factories soon cropped up along what was becoming a major trade hub.

Manhattanville was always a place of commerce, a natural outgrowth of its direct access to river transport and, later, easy access to a west side rail line. Although the meat market flourished in the 1960s and 1970s, in the 1800s one would have already seen a bustling waterfront. In 1965, when my father went looking for goat, there were eighteen meat processing and distribution businesses in Manhattanville. These markets were simply part of the mix and continuum of trade that had flourished in the area for generations.

Manhattanville meat market captured in
Under Riverside Drive Viaduct, 125th Street at
12th Avenue, Manhattan, Berenice Abbott,
1931. Courtesy of the New York Public Library.

In the 1920s, as part of the West Side Improvement Project, the New York Central railway's tracks were rebuilt as an underground cut through Riverside Park and were raised onto a viaduct between West 123rd Street and West 137th Street. Meat, dairy, and other industries built elevators to transport the freight from the elevated rails down to the warehouses and industries located along the west side of Twelfth Avenue. As a result of these transportation improvements, industry along the Twelfth Avenue corridor continued to thrive into the 1940s and 1950s.[6]

My father remembered going by ferry from the foot of 125th Street to Edgewater, New Jersey, as late as 1950. Ferry service had begun in 1809 between New Jersey and a bulkhead at the foot of West 130th (now 125th) Street. New Jersey towns along the Hudson hosted the burgeoning motion picture industry until the move to more sunny climes in California. At one time, Fort Lee was the movie capital of America. The industry got its start at the end of the nineteenth century with the construction of Thomas Edison's Black Maria studios in West Orange. Land in the cities and towns on the New Jersey coast was cheaper than New York City property across the river, and the area flourished.

Kalem Company began using Fort Lee in 1907 as a location for filming in the area, and other filmmakers quickly followed. In 1909, a forerunner of Universal Studios, the Champion Film Company, built the first studio. That company was quickly followed by others who either built new studios or leased facilities in Fort Lee. In the 1910s and 1920s, film companies such as the Independent Moving Pictures Company, Peerless Studios, the Solax Company, and others were launching successful film projects in New Jersey and taking the Fort Lee ferry to go home to their families or to enjoy the Roaring Twenties in Manhattan. However, shortly thereafter film studios began moving to California. The weather was better, and they were able to avoid the fees imposed by Thomas Edison, who owned multiple patents on the moviemaking process.[7]

If you pay close attention to a map of Manhattanville or stroll its streets you'll find echoes of this history. Tiemann Street, just south of 125th Street between Broadway and Riverside Drive, was named after Daniel F. Tiemann (1805–1899), owner of the D. F. Tiemann & Company Color Works. Tiemann, arguably Manhattanville's most famous citizen, served as Mayor of New York from 1858 to 1859 and his considerable enterprise consisted of about a dozen buildings between Manhattan and 127th Streets. As Tiemann surveyed his holdings, he would have also seen icehouses, stables, and warehouses stuffed with goods, as well as an active ferry terminal.[8]

In 1851 the Hudson River Railroad was completed, connecting Manhattanville to Manhattan in the south, and in 1865 a streetcar line was inaugurated, allowing passengers to travel to "the city" in a speedy one and a half hours. Automobile finishing plants were established during the early part of the twentieth century. The Nash

6 New York City Department of Planning, "Proposed Manhattanville in West Harlem Rezoning and Academic Mixed-Use Development FEIS," Chapter 8: Historic Resources, November 2007, 8.

7 Charles E. Pedersen, *Thomas Edison* (Edina, MN: ABDO Publishing, 2007), 77.

8 Washington, *Manhattanville*, 84.

Motor and Studebaker Buildings still stand in Manhattanville. The Studebaker Building, located at 615 West 131st Street between Broadway and Twelfth Avenue, was constructed in 1923.[9] Constructed largely of brick with a decorative white porcelain trim, it is six stories tall, and the blue Studebaker logo used between 1912 and 1934 is still visible on the southwest corner near the top. Although the last Studebaker automobiles ceased being manufactured in 1966, and Nash ended as a brand a decade earlier, the building names still resonate.

As important as these industries were, though, some would say that they associate Manhattanville not with automobiles or slabs of meat, but with milk. By the late 1800s almost all of Manhattan's milk supply was arriving by railroad and the 130th Street railroad station became an important hub. In fact, in 1937 Studebaker sold its building to the Borden Company, which used it as a milk-processing plant.[10]

In the 1820s and 1830s, as New York City grew, imaginative entrepreneurs brought cows into the city not to "graze on the village green" but to eat grain mash left over from the distilling process. Breweries sold this "swill" as cattle feed. Farmers rented stalls at the distillery and fed their cows at minimal cost. Of course the milk was of poor quality, thanks in part to what the cattle were fed but also because the animals lived in filthy conditions. The thin, poor quality milk might then be doctored with additives such as plaster or chalk to give it a whiter color. According to statistics, in 1841 half of children in the city died before the age of five, many from milk-borne diseases.[11]

In 1910 two local women, Ethel M. Wagoner Hooke and Minnie M. Cook, both residents of 552 Riverside Drive in Manhattanville, founded the International Pure Milk League, devoted "to the investigation of problems in connection with the production of clean, pure milk at prices within the reach of persons of moderate means."[12] In 1912, in part due to the league's activism, New York City decreed that all milk sold to children should be pasteurized.[13]

In 1909 the Sheffield Farms building, located at 632 West 125th Street (now Columbia's Prentis Hall), was a milk pasteurization and bottling facility. Sheffield Farms' large window-wall facade facing 125th Street served to demystify this strange new pasteurization process. Passersby were to able see into the plant and watch the treated milk flow into clear glass containers; workers dressed in white coveralls to underscore the purity of the process. The manufacturer encouraged residents to enter the building and constructed an interior balcony that allowed the viewer to look even more deeply into its workings. The area became a center of milk processing, and Sheffield Farms was joined in Manhattanville by Borden Condensed Milk and McDermott-Bunger Dairy.[14]

As I mentioned, another important food industry in Manhattanville was meat. Although it was primarily a wholesale

9 *Wikipedia*, s.v. "Studebaker Building (Columbia University)," https://en.wikipedia.org/wiki/Studebaker_Building_(Columbia_University).

10 Ben Huff, "Manhattanville's History and Development in Harlem," *Untapped Cities*, February 26, 2013, http://untappedcities.com/2013/02/26/manhattanville-history-and-development/.

11 Mary Habstritt, "Manhattanville and New York City's Milk Supply," *Gray Wolf's Howl* blog, February 13, 2008, http://reysmont.blogspot.com/2008/02/manhattanville-and-new-york-citys-milk.html.

12 "Pure Milk League Formed by Women of New York," *Los Angeles Herald*, September 8, 1910.

13 Habstritt, "Manhattanville and New York City's Milk Supply.

14 Habstritt, "Manhattanville and New York City's Milk Supply.

The Studebaker Building, c. 1940, when it
was used as a milk processing plant by the
Borden Company. Courtesy of Columbia
University Facilities.

operation, my father was not the only immigrant who traveled by subway to Twelfth Avenue for a taste of a homeland that he would never return to. While in some ways the 1974 opening of the Hunts Point wholesale meat market accelerated the decline of the Manhattanville meat processing and wholesale distribution industries, arguably the decline had begun as early as the 1960s. Formal censure in the early 1980s by the federal Food and Drug Administration cited unsafe and unsanitary conditions in the market and stated that they would have to clean up their act, literally. Realizing that such modernization was going to be costly, the merchants turned to city government for help.

The city did not want to lose these important jobs, especially in an era of deindustrialization. However, they had already poured big dollars into infrastructure improvements at a meat and produce facility in the Hunts Point section of the Bronx. Hunts Point, one of the largest food-distribution centers in the world, covered 329 acres; the Meat Distribution Center opened along the Bronx River in 1974, on land the city leased to the Hunts Point Cooperative Market Inc. City leaders wanted to geographically consolidate this industry and told the Manhattanville meat-market owners and vendors that they would assist them with grants and low-cost loans but only if they moved to the new Bronx center.

Over the years, even before this policy mandate, low-wage jobs in moving and storage, wholesale industrial supply, parking lots, garages, and auto repair industries had begun to take over from market and industry. According to a 1984 planning study conducted for the Harlem Urban Development Corporation (HUDC), in 1965 the area that roughly corresponds to Columbia's Manhattanville campus site contained 111 firms employing a total of 5,395 people; by 1984 there were 91 firms employing 1,916 people. Highlights of the decline include a reduction in the number of manufacturing businesses from nineteen to three, a decline in meat wholesalers from eighteen to eleven, and a decline in the number of active warehouses from nine to three, echoing a trend found in American cities, and cities all over the developed world.

Local elected officials led by Congressman Charles Rangel saw these trends and worked with the HUDC to obtain funds to support a planning study to see how the area could be redeveloped. I had been working as head of planning and development for then Borough President David Dinkins, but in 1988 I had stepped down from that post, lured by a project in St. Thomas, Virgin Islands. The project stalled after a few months; when I returned, I was available to work with the planning firm Abeles Phillips Preiss & Shapiro, which had been asked to develop a plan for Manhattanville. They were not the first to attempt this; an earlier proposal had recommended a mixed-use development that would have included four market-rate residential towers and a marina.[15] However, as one can imagine, this scenario proved unacceptable to both

15 "Japanese Companies May Join in Big Harlem Waterfront Development Plan," *Los Angeles Times*, January 22, 1988; Mariann Yen, "Japanese Mull Investment in Harlem," *Washington Post*, February 21, 1989; Lucia Mouat, "Restoring Harlem to Former Glory: Long-Troubled Cultural Capital of Black America Is Attracting Big Plans, Including Marina," *Christian Science Monitor*, January 14, 1992.

16 Jessica Goodheart, "Harlem Leaders Critical of Hudson Development," *Columbia Daily Spectator*, November 12, 1987; Alex Roth, "A Community Divides Over Harlem on the Hudson," *Columbia Daily Spectator*, November 13, 1989.

17 Abeles Philips Preiss & Shapiro, Inc., "Harlem on the Hudson Feasibility Study," submitted to the New York City Economic Development Corporation, the Harlem Urban Development Corporation, and the New York State Urban Development Corporation, July 1992.

18 Abeles Philips Preiss & Shapiro, "Harlem on the Hudson Feasibility Study."

19 Columbia's engineers and construction team designed and built a 240-foot-deep watertight perimeter diaphragm slurry wall to keep water out of the Manhattanville site. See Seifert Associates website, http://www.siefertassociates.com/projects/columbia-university.

government and community leaders.[16] Then as now, community residents and their elected leadership resisted the concept of housing whose units would not have been affordable to the current residents; it's also doubtful that Harlemites considered establishment of a marina a high priority. Perhaps the more critical issue was the question of jobs and whether the proposed development would truly generate the number and the kind of jobs community residents desired.

The Abeles Phillips analysis focused on the area's unique qualities, citing the unusual topography and the fact that Manhattanville exists in a valley surrounded by hills, and that this led to extraordinary "architectural elements … the three elevated structures spanning the hills."[17] The report also heralded Manhattanville as the only place above midtown where the "streets lead directly to the waterfront, without the need to cross a highway or railroad tracks." To celebrate this accident of geography the report recommended the establishment of a waterfront promenade. Otherwise, the plan focused on a creative but time-honored economic development approach, including introducing a new, consolidated meat market facility, food and flower markets, traditional retail, and arts-oriented uses that acknowledged the area's heritage.[18] This approach was much more acceptable to government and community leadership. However, given the lack of a strong Harlem real estate market in the 1990s, potential developers did not seem willing to undertake a project with what would have been extremely high development costs. Construction costs would have been especially dear given high water tables in the area and the need for advanced and expensive below-grade construction techniques.[19]

In 1989, I was working for Abeles Phillips on the preliminary Harlem on the Hudson planning study, interviewing stakeholders, taking photographs, and becoming familiar with "existing conditions," when the fact that I was raised as an Episcopalian led me to a serendipitous but significant Manhattanville friendship.

While some of our American brethren traded incense and wafers for guitars and bagels during service, we West Indian Episcopalians were originalists and held fast to the old ways. That's why I found myself at 521 West 126th Street, after a couple of glasses of spiked punch, singing old time Episcopal hymns at a fundraiser held in the basement of St. Mary's Episcopal Church, Manhattanville. On the St. Mary's website you find the following introduction:

> On Thanksgiving Day, celebrated in 1823 on December 18th, leaders within a rural community holding promise of becoming a thriving village, met in the local school house run by the Finlays, for the

Construction underway at the Sheffield
Farms milk bottling facility on 125th Street
and Twelfth Avenue, c. 1910. Photograph
from *Architecture and Building*, v. 43.

purpose of organizing a church. St. Michael's, an Episcopal Parish to the south, provided encouragement and support. The name selected for the new parish was St. Mary's Church, Manhattanville, in the Ninth Ward of the City of New York. Valentine Nutter and Jacob Schieffelin were chosen as Wardens, and among the first Vestrymen of the newly formed church was also Jacob's son, Richard L. Schieffelin.[20]

St. Mary's is also where I met Rev. Robert Wilkinson Castle Jr. Father Castle was a priest, activist, and, oddly enough, also an actor.[21] At the time of our meeting, Castle was trying to decide whether to submit St. Mary's three-building complex for designation as a New York City Landmark. After finding out that I was a city planner with a degree in architecture and a familiarity with his church, he asked if I would take on a pre-decision study of the buildings. He wanted to know the pros and cons, the added costs of maintaining preservation-designated buildings, what grants or low-interest loans might be available, and so on. He also wanted to upgrade the basement for use as a Pre-K facility. We completed the study in record time; he was pleased and subsequently decided to apply for designation.[22]

Father Castle and I became friends, and I, a lapsed Episcopalian, was often in his little sitting room in the vestry, sometimes joined by his artist wife, listening as he railed against the 26th Police Precinct across the street, where officers parked illegally in front of the church, taking places away from parishioners. He also talked about his work with the Black Panthers and his "exile," when church leadership had thought that they were punishing him by putting him in a small Harlem church, though in fact he loved the place and its people very much.

Castle was wary about the plan for the area; he feared gentrification and was mistrustful of government plans in general. However, he loved to talk about his church, and it was from Father Castle that I first heard of the church's long and distinguished history. In 2000 Father Castle retired to Vermont, where he died in 2012.

After multiple presentations and years of drafts, planning studies, preliminary reports and fine-tuning, the Harlem on the Hudson Feasibility Study was eventually published in the summer of 1992. By that time Mayor David Dinkins had appointed me to the New York City Planning Commission, and I had withdrawn from the project because of concern about a possible conflict of interest were the plan to come before the commission. However, during that period, no comprehensive rezoning and development plan based on the Harlem on the

20 "A Brief History of St. Mary's Episcopal Church, Manhattanville," *St. Mary's Episcopal Church, Harlem Blog*, December 2011, https://stmarysharlem.wordpress.com/history/.

21 Castle was the subject of the 1992 documentary film *Cousin Bobby*, directed by his cousin and film director Jonathan Demme. His involvement in Demme's documentary led to an unlikely career as an actor in more than a dozen films over the next two decades, including a role in the Academy Award-winning film *Philadelphia*, as well as in *The Addiction*, *Beloved*, and *Rachel Getting Married*. See Wikipedia, s.v. "Robert W. Castle," https://en.wikipedia.org/wiki/Robert_W._Castle.

22 The formal landmark preservation process was led by historian and author Eric K. Washington.

Hudson report was ever formally submitted for review. There was, however, incremental progress.

In 1994 Manhattanville was designated part of the Upper Manhattan Empowerment Zone. This designation brought with it eligibility for certain tax incentives and investment. In 1995, Fairway, a wholesale/retail food market, opened on Twelfth Avenue and 133rd Street, and in 1998 the Department of Parks and Recreation constructed Cherry Walk, a West Side riverfront walk and bikeway along the river's edge ending just to the south of the Harlem Piers. Also in 1998, West Harlem Environmental Action, Inc. (WE ACT) received a grant from the US Department of Energy to develop a community-based vision in partnership with Community Board 9 for the Harlem Piers area.[23] That vision became a reality when West Harlem Piers Park was opened in the spring of 2009.

23   West Harlem Environmental Action, "Harlem Group Applauds Selection of Community Vision as Benchmark for Harlem Piers Redevelopment," February 1, 2001, http://old.weact.org/pressadvisories/2001_Feb_1.html.

In 1996 I resigned from the Planning Commission to take a position at the US Department of Housing and Urban Development. In 1999, I left my position there, to come teach at Columbia University's Graduate School of Architecture, Planning, and Preservation. At the same time, my friend and colleague (the current New York City Parks Commissioner) Mitchell Silver was working with Abeles Phillips Preiss & Shapiro to develop a new plan for Manhattanville. The plan, driven this time by the local community board, was known as Harlem on the River. Silver asked if he could pick my brain informally, and also whether I would help coordinate a daylong session to solicit community input. I was happy to do this and ended up leading the discussion at a table that included Patricia Jones, a dynamic financial professional and community leader whom I would meet again in 2005 when she and Donald Notice led community benefits negotiations on behalf of her West Harlem community.

In 2000, Community Board 9 endorsed the Harlem on the River plan, and the city's Economic Development Corporation issued a request for proposals for development. However, in the end, they did not move forward with the plan, although much was learned from this and earlier efforts and many of its concepts were incorporated into subsequent efforts.

In 2005, while I was in Philadelphia serving as deputy mayor and head of city planning, a friend told me that she had been contacted by an executive search firm about a job at Columbia University. She said that Columbia wanted to establish a campus on the waterfront in West Harlem and asked hadn't I already done some planning work in Manhattanville? Even after learning more about this project, which played to my interests and strengths—navigation of the city's byzantine land use process and community outreach, and the need to work closely with two extraordinary design firms—I was hesitant to move. Mayor John Street in Philadelphia had only recently been re-elected and there was a lot more good work to be done there. In the end, though, I thought about going home. I thought about Harlem, about the goat meat that my father had chosen with care, but that I refused to eat. I thought about the ride on the A train, where I was allowed to buy, against my mother's strict directive, a Baby Ruth bar and a comic book for the trip; I considered my planning work with colleagues, interviewing people who worked for less than minimum wage in auto-repair shops. I thought about singing hymns with Father Castle and about old men sitting on the edge of the West Harlem Piers with ancient fishing poles. I also thought that after all of those studies and meetings and community board votes and government interventions, a university, a neighbor, might be willing to finally help breathe life into an old industrial neighborhood with a long and proud history and I was homesick. So when asked if I was at all familiar with Harlem's Manhattanville neighborhood, of course I said, "Yes, I am."

2000

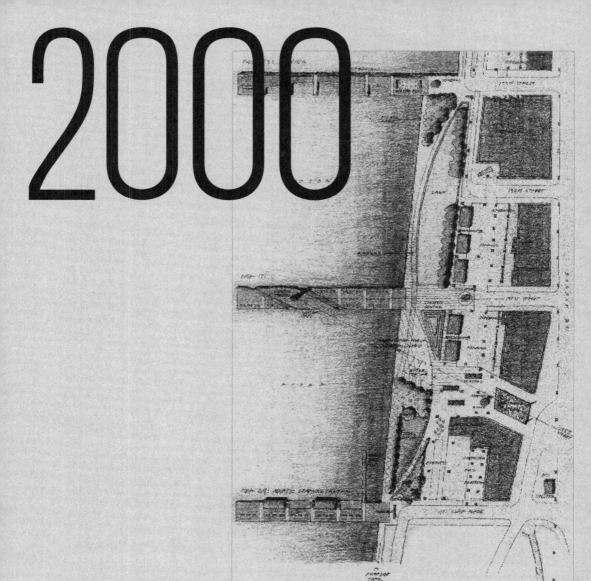

Harlem on the River plan developed through the community planning process, published in 2004. Courtesy of WE ACT for Environmental Justice.

Artist rendering of waterfront path, published in 2004. Courtesy of WE ACT for Environmental Justice.

Harlem on the River

The West Harlem Piers Park opened in 2009. However, the waterfront as we know it today is largely the product of the Harlem on the River project initiated by West Harlem Environmental Action (WE ACT). In 1998, funded by a grant from the U.S. Department of Energy, WE ACT and Community Board 9 responded to a request for proposals issued by the New York City Economic Development Corporation (EDC) for the development of Harlem Piers.[1] The resulting project positioned itself both as a way to ameliorate decades of disinvestment and neglect in West Harlem and as a defense against future policy failures like those that had caused the environmental injustices and health disparities suffered by the community. In many ways, Harlem on the River was also a reaction against numerous revitalization efforts since the 1970s, including the Harlem Urban Development Corporation's Harlem on the Hudson, which together had imagined a waterfront complete with hotels, marina and ferry service, market-rate housing developments, high-tech telecommunications establishments, cinemas, and entertainment and sports venues.[2] As WE ACT lamented, "Outsiders were designing, refining, configuring, contorting our dream. Like well-intentioned sandmen, developers, elected officials,

and city agencies who were breezing into Harlem, impoverishing our imagination, pinching our ownership of the process, handing us their dream."[3]

Inverting the historical model of development in Harlem, WE ACT and Community Board 9 mobilized community residents and stakeholders, positioning them at the center of the planning process. Urban planner Mitchell Silver, of Abeles Phillips Preiss & Shapiro, was contracted to help facilitate the design process, which consisted of a series of community-wide meetings and open design charrettes and workshops. At these events, the myriad voices, opinions, and interests of the community were synthesized into composite images and maps of the future that outlined planning philosophies, offered key recommendations, and presented sketches of new realities. Together with the help of a steering committee established by WE ACT— composed of community residents, elected officials, community leaders, and local business and community-based academic institutions— Silver and his team of design professionals produced a final comprehensive concept plan.

This community-driven plan presented West Harlem as the northernmost portion of a continuous greenway starting in Battery Park and stretching along the Hudson. Harlem on the River produced a

comprehensive list of demands and recommendations across seven categories, including job creation, riverfront access, transportation, arts and culture, streetscape improvement, environmental restoration, and history. It proposed an eighteen-hour commercial corridor that consisted of daytime and after-hour retail businesses, a wider riverfront park space for passive recreation, and restored piers for ferry service and water-related activities—not to mention recommending public parking underneath the viaducts, two-story height limits west of Twelfth Avenue, and new bikeways along the water.[4] In 2000, the EDC announced that it would not move forward with the proposals submitted by private developers but would instead use the Harlem on the River community plan as the benchmark for the master plan and future development of the Harlem Piers.

1
West Harlem Environmental Action, "Harlem Group Applauds Selection of Community Vision as Benchmark for Harlem Piers Redevelopment," February 1, 2001, http://old.weact.org/pressadvisories/2001_Feb_1.html.

2
Harlem on the River: Making a Community Vision Real (New York: WE ACT for Environmental Justice, 2004), 11.

3
Harlem on the River, 15.

4
Harlem on the River, 24.

THE RADIANT
UNIVERSITY:
SPACE, URBAN
REDEVELOPMENT,
AND THE
PUBLIC GOOD

STEVEN GREGORY

One brisk morning in February 2009, a neighbor told me about a rally taking place later that day at La Floridita, a Cuban-owned restaurant in West Harlem. La Floridita was a popular and affordable spot that attracted ethnically diverse customers from the immediate area and beyond. The rally had been organized by Columbia University's Student Coalition on Expansion and Gentrification and was being held to protest the imminent closing and demolition of the restaurant, pursuant to the university's plan to expand its Morningside Heights campus into a 17-acre area of West Harlem known as Manhattanville.

The university's $6.7 billion expansion plan called for the acquisition and demolition of all but three buildings in the project's footprint and the construction of a state-of-the-art campus over a roughly thirty-year period. Columbia had been buying properties in Manhattanville for nearly a decade and, in 2004, purchased the squat building at the corner of Broadway and 129th Street that housed La Floridita, an Eritrean social club, and three other commercial tenants. On July 18, 2008, the Empire State Development Corporation (ESDC), a New York State agency charged with promoting economic development, had approved the university's expansion plan and, after determining that Manhattanville was suffering from conditions of "urban blight," cleared the way for the exercise of eminent domain: the state appropriation of private property with compensation for, but without the consent of, property owners.

The use of eminent domain was a lightning rod for community opposition to the expansion plan. Although critics of the plan recognized Columbia's right to expand its campus, they opposed the university's demand for exclusive control of the entire 17-acre project footprint. For its part, the university maintained that the research that would be done at its new campus would serve the public good—directly, by researching cures for illnesses such as Alzheimer's disease, and indirectly, by helping to usher the city into a knowledge-based economic future.

The protest was to take the form of a walking tour of the project site. Three community activists who had been staunch opponents of the university's expansion would lead the tour: Nellie Bailey, president of the Harlem Tenants Council, a community-based tenants rights organization; Vicky Gholson, a member of West Harlem's Community Board 9, which had opposed the campus expansion plan; and Mario Mazzoni, an activist working with the Coalition to Preserve Community, a community organization that had been formed in 2002 to resist the expansion plan.

Once the crowd had gathered on 129th Street, Gholson raised her bullhorn and directed the group to make its way to a gas station located further along the triangular shaped block. The station was one of two in the area owned by Gurnam Singh and his wife, Parminder Kaur, immigrants from Punjab. The couple had started the Manhattanville businesses twenty-five years earlier.[1] In 2009, Singh was one of two property owners who had refused to sell to the university. The other owners, whose buildings housed a motley assortment of car repair shops, meat wholesalers, and small manufacturing shops, had already sold their properties to the university—according to some, under considerable pressure. The second holdout, Nick Sprayregen, owned Tuck-It-Away, a self-storage company occupying three large buildings within the proposed project's footprint.

1   Timothy Williams, "2 Gas Stations, and a Family's Resolve, Confront Columbia Expansion Plan," *New York Times*, September 20, 2008.

At each stop along the tour—a large self-storage facility, a booming barbeque restaurant, and two recently renovated apartment buildings—Gholson, Bailey, and Mazzoni talked about the site's history and context, challenging the ESDC's finding that the neighborhood was "blighted" and the university's characterization of the area as an "obsolete" former manufacturing district. At a car repair shop, Mazzoni paused and raised his bullhorn. The repair shop was bustling with activity. Cars in various states of repair filled the garage and curbside parking spaces. A half dozen or so mechanics looked on with curiosity. "This is a good example of the kind of business that Columbia says is blighting the area. But this repair shop provides good jobs and provides a service that people in the community need. Why should Columbia, using the threat of eminent domain, have the power to decide what the needs of this community are? Or determine which jobs and businesses are valuable and worth saving?"

In the debates surrounding Columbia University's expansion plan and the state's approval of the use of eminent domain, Columbia and its supporters depicted Manhattanville as an obsolete, former manufacturing district no longer capable of contributing to the city's economy—an area lacking in vitality and stalled in time. To support this narrative, the project's boosters mustered a visual rhetoric that stoked modernist anxieties about chaotic urbanism and the disorderly street. In alignment with these concerns, the project's designers proffered a symbolic economy rooted in an aesthetic of "transparency," a symbolic economy that they maintained was better suited to the city's postindustrial future.

This discourse of transparency—framed as a solution to urban blight—elided the asymmetrical power relations that underpin urban land use decisions and, as a result, masked the social consequences of elite-driven development policies. A critical analysis of these discourses and their related practices can shed light on the spatial ideologies that are mobilized to support neoliberal development strategies. Just as economic neoliberalism imagines "free" markets unencumbered by state regulation, this discourse of transparency evoked a spatial economy unencumbered by history, unblemished by the spatialized interests, practices, and struggles of the past.

THE BUILD-UP

In the fall of 2003, Columbia announced its plan to expand its Morningside Heights campus into Manhattanville. Public and private planners had long recognized the area's potential for redevelopment due to its extraordinary access to subway, rail, and water transportation, and to the Henry Hudson Parkway. As early as 1991, West Harlem's Community Board 9 had begun preparing a comprehensive redevelopment plan for the area pursuant to Section 197-a of the New York City Charter.[2] Community Board 9's redevelopment plan underscored Manhattanville's potential for creating jobs and business opportunities that would benefit the residents of West Harlem.

In August of 2002, the New York City Economic Development Corporation (EDC) published the West Harlem Master Plan for the redevelopment of Manhattanville. The plan was informed by EDC consultations with an array of community organizations and local businesses. A key long-term objective of the master plan was the creation of an "intermodal hub" that would improve public transportation access to Manhattanville and the piers area. This plan included extending bus service to Twelfth Avenue, establishing ferry service to the recreation pier, and building a Metro-North station at 125th Street, thus restoring the area's link to rail service along the Hudson River.

Although the master plan envisioned the growth of "multiple uses and a mixture of new and existing jobs," a goal that suggested broad community participation during the plan's implementation, the EDC had already ceded "lead responsibility" to Columbia for the institutional and economic redevelopment of the area, and "joint lead responsibility" with the EDC for its necessary rezoning. In January 2003, the university submitted the Columbia master plan to the EDC, which asserted the university's *exclusive* control over the Manhattanville industrial area. Columbia officials claimed that exclusive control was necessary in order to construct a "bathtub" below the site: a seven-story subterranean basement that would conceal the new campus's infrastructure and enable pedestrian traffic between buildings.[3] In that same year, the EDC included in its plan documents supporting the exercise

2   New York City is divided into fifty-nine community boards. Each is composed of up to fifty members appointed by the board's borough president. Manhattan Community Board 9 encompasses the area from 110th Street to 155th Street on the west side of Manhattan, including the neighborhoods of Morningside Heights, Manhattanville, and Hamilton Heights. Though the community boards review urban land use decisions, their role is merely advisory.

3   The 80-foot-deep bathtub stirred controversy among opponents of the expansion on environmental grounds. Some argued that, given the project footprint's location in a potential flood zone, the bathtub and facilities that it contained would be vulnerable to storm surge flooding. Columbia geophysicist Klaus Jacob, a respected authority on urban environmental issues, warned Columbia officials that a storm surge, worsened by the effects of climate change, could lead to a wide-scale disaster. According to Jacob his concerns went unheeded. "My original concern was to help Columbia solve its own problem," he told the *Village Voice.* "But for some reason, they weren't interested. I was naïve enough to think that by mentioning something, I could make something happen' (*Village Voice,* October 1, 2008; see also *Columbia Spectator,* November 30, 2008).

Rally at Singh and Kaur's gas station, Manhattanville, February 2009. Photograph by the author.

Harlem Tenants Council supporters march to Nos Quedamos rally, Harlem, February 2009. Photograph by the author.

of condemnation proceedings in Manhattanville, pursuant to the city's Eminent Domain Procedure Law (EDPL §207). To that purpose, the EDC retained the consulting firm Urbitran Associates Inc. to determine whether or not Manhattanville was "blighted"—a prerequisite for the approval of eminent domain. In 2004, the ESDC, the only state agency empowered to approve eminent domain, began promoting the Columbia master plan, convening a series of meetings with university officials, lawyers, and consultants.

Beginning in 2002, Columbia accelerated its acquisition of properties in Manhattanville; by 2005, the university had acquired twenty-eight of the sixty-seven properties in the area.[4] According to community activists and property owners in Manhattanville, Columbia pressured tenants to vacate university-owned properties and refused to renew leases for longer than one year—a commercially unviable term.

4 James A. Catterson, opinion of the court in *Matter of Tuck-It-Away Associates, L.P. v. Empire State Development Corporation* (July 15, 2008) NY Slip Op 06279 [54 AD3d 154], http://www.courts.state.ny.us/Reporter/3dseries/2008/2008_06279.htm.

HELL NO
WE WON'T GO!

Columbia's proposed expansion into Manhattanville and the state's proceedings to exercise eminent domain did not go unopposed. The Harlem Tenants Council (HTC) convened public meetings and conferences on the Columbia plan, linking the campus expansion to the council's broader stance against gentrification and illegal evictions. The second community-based group, the Coalition to Preserve Community (CPC), had been founded with the express purpose of opposing the Columbia expansion plan. Led by Tom Demott, a Columbia University graduate, the CPC convened local residents, students, members of Community Board 9, and representatives of other groups opposed to the expansion. The group sponsored demonstrations in front of the university and elsewhere, and provided testimony at public hearings.

On Saturday, June 10, 2006, the CPC joined with the HTC and other community groups to march and rally against the gentrification of northern Manhattan and Harlem under the umbrella group Nos Quedamos (Project Remain). Supporters gathered at 9am in Marcus Garvey Park, in central Harlem, where a range of speakers voiced their opposition to tenant evictions, arguing that the university's exclusive control of the Manhattanville site, ensured by the state's impending exercise of eminent domain, was inciting rent hikes and landlord speculation in surrounding neighborhoods.

"Why are we here?" HTC founder Nellie Bailey asked the assembly. "Why are we here? We are here today because, if we don't do something, if we don't organize, Harlem will cease to exist. It will become just a bus stop on tour buses from downtown. Columbia now wants to expand its campus into Manhattanville. And they don't want to work with the community. They have ignored all the proposals that were made by the community board and others.

What they can't buy they are going to take using eminent domain. And we have to stop them!"

After the rally in Marcus Garvey Park, the protestors marched to Broadway and 135th Street, in front of the Riverside Park Community Houses, a 1,192-unit apartment complex that was at the center of an illegal eviction controversy. Many community activists believed that the rent increases and evictions at Riverside Park had been provoked by the Columbia expansion plan since the apartment complex bordered on the project footprint.

As the marchers chanted "Hell no we won't go!," Rosalind, a middle-aged African-American woman, expressed her thoughts about the Columbia expansion. "This is nothing new," she began. "Columbia has been running roughshod over Harlem for years. In 1968, they tried to build a gym in Morningside Park on public land! And the community stopped them. Now they want to take all this," she said, gesturing to the project footprint with a sweep of her arm. "And they don't want to give the community any say at all."

Riverside Park Community Houses was completed in 1976, using subsidies made available by the Mitchell-Lama Housing Program, a New York State program established in 1955 that provided low-interest mortgages and property tax exemptions to developers in return for commitments to provide housing at below-market rents. In 2005, the housing complex's owner, Jerome Belson, opted out of the program by prepaying the subsidized mortgage. This enabled him to adjust rents to market levels. As a result, many tenants saw their rents skyrocket while maintenance services were neglected. Many community activists and tenants of the complex believed that Belson's decision to leave Mitchell-Lama was influenced by the Columbia expansion plan and the promise of rising property values.

However successful the rally was, the broad-based and improvised Nos Quedamos coalition, though demonstrating the potential power of the public, was too unwieldy and unfocussed to engage effectively in the drawn-out and often opaque process of the project's public review. The protracted road to approval required the rezoning of the project area (i.e., from light manufacturing to mixed-use), review and approval of the project's environmental impact statement and general project plan, and a decision by the ESDC approving the use of eminent domain. At each step along the process, public hearings were held before such entities as Community Board 9, the City Planning Commission, the Manhattan Borough President and, in the end, the New York City Council. However, community input at these public hearings was restricted: public comments were typically limited to two minutes, and the opinions and judgments expressed by speakers were merely advisory.

On March 8, 2006, Lee Bollinger, president of Columbia University, appeared on the Brian Lehrer Show, a radio talk show broadcast on public radio station WNYC. The subject was the university's expansion plan. Midway through the interview, Lehrer asked President Bollinger about the possible use of eminent domain, to which Bollinger replied:

State Assemblyman Adriano Espaillat interviewed in front of the Riverside Park Community Houses, February 2009. Photograph by the author.

Post-demolition construction begins at Columbia's Manhattanville campus, 2011. Photograph by the author.

Eminent domain is itself a part of our constitutional system to help achieve public purposes and, if we want to build a national park and private property stands in the way, it's very important for the collective good that we be able to have eminent domain. Columbia is a nonprofit, public institution. It's not a private developer. We're not trying to make money, and if a party stands in the way of developing neuroscience work, which may actually find a cure to Alzheimer's—the second gene to Alzheimer's was just discovered by a Columbia scientist—that is a proper use of eminent domain.

To which Lehrer replied that in fact, Columbia is not a public institution like, say SUNY but rather a not-for-profit, private institution.[5]

Eminent domain, and the justification of its use, stoked community opposition to the Columbia expansion plan. Although Community Board 9 recognized the university's right to expand its campus, it opposed Columbia's demand for exclusive control of the project's footprint. Moreover, some argued, Columbia's expanded campus would serve a private and not "public use," as required by the state constitution for the exercise of eminent domain. For its part, the university maintained that the research done on the expanded campus would serve the public good—generating jobs and "maintaining Upper Manhattan as a world center for knowledge, creativity, and solutions for society's challenges."[6]

The university's assertion that the campus expansion would contribute to the public good was rooted in broader claims in the media and academic literature about the increasing importance of the "knowledge economy" in producing economic growth in postindustrial cities. A concept that was first popularized by Peter Drucker in his book *The Age of Discontinuity* (1969), the knowledge economy has generally been used to refer to the use of knowledge technologies—often, information and communication technologies—and knowledge-intensive activities to produce job creation and economic development.

Key to the concept is the claim that under postindustrial conditions, intellectual capabilities have become more important to producing economic growth than physical inputs and natural resources associated with the manufacturing sector.[7] However, some critics have argued that the rise of the knowledge industry is a presumption rather than an empirically established fact since "the stock of knowledge embodied in production is difficult to measure and compare across time."[8]

The appeal to the knowledge economy made it possible for Columbia to construct the public good in abstract and future-oriented terms—for example, the often cited promise of a cure for Alzheimer's disease—while ignoring, if not discounting, the needs and aspirations of surrounding communities. Before the courts, public officials, and much

5   *The Brian Lehrer Show*, WNYC, July 3, 2008.

6   "Neighbors," Columbia University website, http://www.columbia.edu/content/neighbors.html.

7   Walter W. Powell and Kaisa Snellman, "The Knowledge Economy," *Annual Review of Sociology* 30 (2004): 199–220.

8   C. P. Chandrasekhar, "Who Needs a 'Knowledge Economy'?: Information, Knowledge and Flexible Labor," *Social Scientist*, vol. 34, no. 1 (2006): 70–87.

of the public, the appeal to the knowledge economy ultimately provided justification for the exercise of eminent domain.[9]

TRANSPARENCY AND THE FUTURE OF THE CITY

In September 2006, the ESDC entered into contract with AKRF, Inc., a planning and engineering consulting firm, to conduct a neighborhood conditions study to determine whether or not Manhattanville was suffering from "urban blight." If the study determined that blighted conditions existed, the ESDC could approve the use of eminent domain to acquire private properties. In 2004, AKRF had been retained by Columbia to provide assistance in planning the campus expansion and to act as the university's agent in seeking the regulatory approvals necessary for the project. The selection of AKRF to conduct a study that could potentially benefit its client raised serious concerns about the impartiality of its results.

After looking at building conditions, community infrastructure, land use, and environmental conditions, among other factors, AKRF concluded: "Physical conditions in the study area are mainly characterized by aging, poorly maintained, and functionally obsolete industrial buildings, with little indication of recent reinvestment to reverse their generally deteriorated conditions, particularly in industrial properties."[10]

The notion that Manhattanville's buildings and, more generally, the area as a whole were "functionally obsolete" was a leitmotif that ran throughout narratives supporting the university's expansion. This narrative of functional obsolescence—that Manhattanville was temporally locked in its industrial past—was strengthened by the contention that it was physically and "visually isolated" from surrounding neighborhoods. The AKRF study maintained that the project area was isolated from Harlem to the east by the elevated IRT subway viaduct. On the north, the MTA's bus depot separated the study area from the neighborhood of Hamilton Heights. These facilities, the study claimed, impeded, if not blocked, the flow of pedestrian and vehicular traffic through the area. Moreover, AKRF argued that this was "a condition exacerbated by the absence of significant business or recreational destinations within the study area and lack of sidewalk amenities.... The area is essentially treeless, uninviting to pedestrians, and bleak."[11]

This rhetoric of "blockage" and "opacity" was echoed in other planning and publicity documents associated with the expansion plan, and gestured to an anxiety in modernist architecture and urban planning associated with obscure, illegible, and blocked urban spatial forms and relations—qualities of the built environment that formed the discursive foundation of AKRF's Manhattanville analysis.

9   Akin to the concept of the knowledge economy is the notion of the "creative economy" popularized by Richard Florida in his book *The Rise of the Creative Class* (New York: Basic Books, 2002). The core claim advanced by Florida and others is that the creative industries (e.g., advertising, TV and radio, software development, and the arts) have become increasingly important, if not critical, to economic development, or, as Florida put it, "human creativity is the ultimate economic resource" (xiii).

10   AKRF, Inc., "Columbia Manhattanville Neighborhood Conditions Study," November 2007, http://www.esd.ny.gov/Subsidiaries_Projects/Data/Columbia/Additional Resources/Neighborhood Conditions-AKRF/Columbia Manhattanville Neighborhood Conditions-AKRF.html.

11   EarthTech Inc. "Manhattanville Neighborhood Conditions Study," 2008, http://www.empire.state.ny.us/pdf/Columbia Manhattanville/updatedconditions htm, iv.

12   Dorian Davis, "Piano, SOM's Columbia Plan Stirs Controversy," *Architectural Record*, June 18, 2007. Emphasis added.

An article about the campus expansion in *Architectural Record* summed up its architectural vision as conceived by Renzo Piano, one quite opposite the occluded, treeless existing conditions described by AKRF:

> Punctuated by tree-lined quads, his buildings are meant to bring a new, open sense to the neighborhood. Their ground floors will host retail stores and restaurants. "We put the dirty functions—garbage, ramps, parking, and loading—underground, because they make a very *opaque* environment, and we put the research facilities up higher so that everything on the ground is more transparent and public," [Piano] says.[12]

13   "Neighbors," http://neighbors.columbia.edu/pages/manplanning.

14   Iris Young, *Justice and the Politics of Difference* (Princeton: Princeton University Press, 1990), 229.

15   Michel Foucault, "The Eye of Power," in *Power/Knowledge: Selected Interviews, and Other Writings, 1972–1977*, ed. C. Gordon (New York: Pantheon, 1980), 152.

In contrast to its gated Morningside campus, the project's boosters asserted that the glass structures of the new campus would be more accessible and inviting to residents of Harlem and elsewhere. "New buildings will not only be open to the public," the project website claimed, "but will also look and feel open because of transparent glass at the street level."[13] Dirty and disorderly functions, reminiscent of Manhattanville's obsolete past, would be concealed below ground while research functions, oriented toward the future, ascend into the sky. Like Le Corbusier's Radiant City, the new campus design would erase the present in order to discard history and annul memory.

If the rhetoric of transparency promised deliverance from the area's murky industrial past toward a radiant economic future, then it also proposed a utopian ideal of community, "an urge to unity," as Iris Young put it, in which the self is transparent to the self and to others.[14] Michel Foucault, noting the complementary relation between the "Rousseauist dream" and Jeremy Bentham's Panopticon schema and its will to "universal transparency," explained:

> It was the dream of a transparent society, visible and legible in each of its parts, the dream of there no longer existing any zones of darkness, zones established by the privileges of royal power or the prerogative of some corporation, zones of disorder. It was the dream that each individual, whatever position he occupied, might be able to see the whole of society, that men's hearts should communicate, their vision unobstructed by obstacles, and that the opinion of all reign over each.[15]

This ideal of transparency and the more strategic claim that glass architecture would "look and feel open" to residents of Harlem and elsewhere not only privileged vision as a way of comprehending the world but also elided the complex, historically constituted relations of power that existed between the university and its surrounding neighborhoods and, more generally, northern Manhattan—asymmetrical power relations that yield varied consequences to the act of "being seen." Like Bentham's quest for universal transparency through the carceral Panopticon, the glass campus would render the street and public space more vulnerable to surveillance than the research laboratories housed inside. Far from welcoming social differences, this will to transparency "represses the ontological difference of subjects," as Iris Young put it, discounting asymmetries in the effects of visibility between those who exercise power and those who are subject to its gaze.[16]

Indeed, although the project's plan promised openness and transparency, its progress through the complex process of public approval had been far from transparent. For example, the neighborhood conditions study failed to report that the west side of Twelfth Avenue (excluded from the study) had been undergoing something of an urban renaissance. More generally, as Tuck-it-Away's 2009 petition to the Appellate Division of the New York State Supreme Court against the ESDC argued, the AKRF report was bereft of any economic analysis of the area.

In 1995, Fairway, a 35,000-square-foot supermarket, opened on Twelfth Avenue in a former meat packing plant. A combination gourmet and wholesale food store, Fairway boasted a 250-car parking lot and drew customers from as far away as New Jersey and Westchester County.[17] Fairway's success attracted visitors and other businesses to the area. In 2004, Dinosaur Bar-B-Que opened on the east side of Twelfth Avenue at 131st Street. The popular restaurant featured live music and attracted throngs of customers from Harlem, Washington Heights, and as far away as Connecticut. Soon afterward, a plumbing contractor bought an abandoned railroad freight warehouse on the west side of Twelfth Avenue, just north of the Columbia project area and leased the 20,900-square-foot building to restaurateurs, prompting the *New York Times* to describe the area as an emerging "restaurant row."[18] In this light, the AKRF study's assertion in 2007 that pedestrian and vehicular traffic to the area was "impeded" by the MTA bus terminal and by the Broadway subway viaduct, and worsened by a lack of "significant destinations," was dubious at best.

The neighborhood conditions study also noted that 72 percent of the properties surveyed were either owned by or under contract to Columbia, leading critics of the expansion to charge that the university had been complicit in their deterioration. In fact, of the eighteen color photographs documenting blight presented in the study's "Current Conditions" section, all but two were taken in properties owned by the university at the time of the study's release on November 1, 2007. The coincidence of neglect, underutilization, and "lack of transparency" with Columbia ownership prompted critics of the project to charge that the university was itself responsible for the "blight" since, in many cases, their vacant status and underutilization was a consequence of their purchase by the university.

16 Young, *Justice and the Politics of Difaference*, 230

17 "Fairway Draws Crowds to Harlem," *Columbia University Record*, vol. 21, no. 17 (1996).

18 Alison Gregor "Square Feet: Along a Viaduct, a Restaurant Row Emerges," *New York Times*, June 7, 2007.

As a member of Harlem's Community Board 9 put it to me, "Columbia has basically blighted the neighborhood by buying it up and by keeping most of what they bought vacant. You know, the life was drained out of the neighborhood. A whole lot of what was going on in the footprint, economic activity, social life, is no longer going on. It's a dead zone."

On March 3, 2007, the West Harlem Business Group, a coalition of Manhattanville property owners who had resisted the university's efforts to buy their properties, filed an Article 78, Freedom of Information Law, petition in the New York State Supreme Court. The petition, alleging that the ESDC had colluded with the university by hiring AKRF, sought the release of relevant ESDC documents. On June 27, 2007, state supreme court judge Shirley Werner Kornreich ordered the ESDC to release 117 documents and items of correspondence that shed light on the ESDC's relationship to Columbia and AKRF. Justice Kornreich ruled in her decision that "while acting for Columbia, AKRF has an interest of its own in the outcome of respondent's action (i.e., the ESDC's), as AKRF, presumably, seeks to succeed in securing an outcome that its client, Columbia, would favor."[19]

19   *New York Times*, June 30, 2007.

20   Catterson, opinion in *Tuck-It-Away Associates v. Empire State Development Corporation*, 19; emphasis added.

The ESDC appealed the court's FOIL decision, arguing among other things that a "Chinese wall" had been erected between the AKRF team working for the ESDC, and the AKRF team working for the university. Consequently, the ESDC argued, AKRF's neighborhood conditions study was not biased toward Columbia's interests. On July 15, 2008, the Appellate Division upheld the earlier court's ruling. Justice James M. Catterson, writing for the majority, concluded:

> It is undisputed that AKRF has worked to promote ESDC's adoption of Columbia's GPP [General Project Plan]. AKRF has been participating in project planning since at least June of 2004 through meetings with ESDC. While in Columbia's employ, AKRF has studied technical, engineering and environmental issues, helping thereby to determine the size, shape and configuration of the proposed project. *AKRF has consistently acted as an advocate for Columbia in seeking ESDC's adoption of Columbia's proposal.*[20]

On July 17, 2008, two days after the ruling, the board of the ESDC met in Manhattan and approved the General Project Plan. In its finding, the ESDC concluded that the project "would maintain the status of the city and New York as centers for higher education, for new graduate programs and scientific research, [and] allow Columbia to maintain its position as one of the foremost educational and cultural institutions in the world."[21] At the meeting, Avi Schick, president and chief operating officer of the ESDC, also announced that the AKRF neighborhood conditions study was not the sole basis for determining that Manhattanville was blighted: a second study had been conducted by a consulting firm not associated with Columbia, which had confirmed ARKF's conclusions. The second study, conducted by EarthTech Inc., had been completed on May 2, 2008, two months before approval of Columbia's General Project Plan.

The EarthTech study further detailed Manhattanville's transparency problem and included an expanded section entitled "Neighborhood Isolation and Visual Conditions." The EarthTech study reiterated the claim that Manhattanville was isolated from Harlem and Hamilton Heights and identified additional barricades (e.g., the Riverside Park Community Houses on the north) that formed "visual barriers" between the study area and surrounding residential communities.[22] To support its account of Manhattanville's "visual clutter" and "grimness," the EarthTech study included photographs of, among other things, cracked sidewalks, windowless building facades, and a dead rat.

AKRF's blight study and EarthTech's subsequent "audit" of its conclusions emphasized the visual and spatial isolation of Manhattanville from surrounding, largely residential areas, suggesting by implication that its razing through the exercise of eminent domain would have few if any consequences beyond its borders. This isolation claim discounted not only the loss of jobs, businesses, and affordable housing that was already occurring as the university acquired properties, but also the impact that the proposed plan would have on affordable housing throughout northern Manhattan. Both neighborhood conditions studies proffered a spatial analysis and ideology that defined old and mixed-use buildings as "streetscape clutter" and the lack of "transparency" as a telltale sign of neighborhood blight and obsolescence. "Although the majority of buildings are low-rise," the EarthTech study opined, "building heights vary, creating a discordant skyline and limit any perception of coherent design."[23]

On August 15, 2007, prior to the release of the AKRF blight study, Community Board 9 held a public hearing on Columbia University's 197-c application to rezone 35 acres of West Harlem, a prerequisite for the approval of the university's General Project Plan The hearing, held at the Manhattanville Community Center, drew a crowd of about three hundred people: representatives of community organizations opposing the expansion plan, and university officials and others supporting the plan, including President Lee Bollinger and former mayor David Dinkins, then a professor at Columbia's School of International and Pubic Affairs. In addition, there were members of a recently formed pro-expansion group, the Coalition for the Future of Manhattanville, which had been organized by Bill Lynch, a paid Columbia consultant (at an estimated $40,000 per month) and Dinkins-era deputy mayor.[24] Lynch had been retained—along with the public relations firm Sunshine Sachs—by the university

21 Alex Philippidis, "NY State's Economic Development Agency OKs Eminent Domain in Columbia Project," *Genomeweb*, December 22, 2008, https://www.genomeweb.com/bioregionnews/ny-state's-economic-development-agency-oks-eminent-domain-columbia-project.

22 EarthTech, "Manhattanville Neighborhood Conditions Study," 2–7.

23 EarthTech, "Manhattanville Neighborhood Conditions Study," 2–11.

24 Juan Gonzale "Rage Building in Harlem," *New York Daily News*, June 1, 2008.

25 *New York Times*, August 16, 2007.

to drum up community support for the expansion plan. The coalition included residents, businesspeople, and others, such as Hazel Dukes, president of the NAACP's New York State Conference, and the Reverend Reginald Williams of Charity Baptist Church in Harlem.[25]

During the five-hour hearing, the *Columbia Spectator* reported that twenty-two people testified in favor of the expansion plan and seventy-three against. Opponents of the plan criticized the university's failure to engage Community Board 9's alternative 197–a plan, as well as its intended resort, via the ESDC, to eminent domain. After the hearing, Community Board 9's Zoning Committee voted 17–1 against the Columbia expansion project, indicating that its support would be withheld unless ten conditions were met, including the construction of low-income housing and the use of higher environmental standards. Five days later, the General Board voted 32–2 in support of the Zoning Committee's earlier vote and ten-point resolution. Following equally contested public hearings, the Department of City Planning approved Columbia's 197–c proposal on November 26, 2007, as did the New York City Council on December 19.

By contrast, the majority of local, citywide, and state-level elected officials supported the expansion plan and the use of eminent domain. Harlem congressman Charles Rangel, state assemblyman Keith L. T. Wright, and city councilman Robert Jackson all expressed their support at key stages in the public review process. Manhattan Borough President Scott Stringer gave his support to the expansion after the university agreed in 2007 to contribute $20 million to start a fund to build affordable housing in the area and provide funds for local parks.[26]

In May 2009, following the approval of the expansion's general project plan by the Public Authorities Control Board (a final benchmark in the approval process), Mayor Michael Bloomberg, whose administration supported large-scale development projects and the use of eminent domain to support private development,[27] and Governor David Patterson issued a joint press release praising the expansion. Mayor Bloomberg's comments echoed the language used by Columbia to promote the project, as well as more general claims about the leading role of the "knowledge economy" in promoting urban economic growth: "Columbia's plan, which was adopted by the City Council in 2007, will transform 17 acres in West Harlem into a modern, academic mixed-use development with 6.8 million square feet of new state-of-the-art facilities that will help solidify New York City as a world-renowned center for higher education and scientific research and enhance New York's ability to attract skilled talent." Governor Patterson, for his part, stressed the benefits for surrounding communities: "The expansion of one of New York's oldest educational institutions will enhance the vitality of both the university and its neighboring community, while meeting the long-term needs of its residents."[28]

26 *New York Times*, September 27, 2007.

27 Julian Brash, *Bloomberg's New York: Class and Governance in the Luxury City* (Athens, GA: University of Georgia Press, 2011).

The only public official to express strong criticism of the project and attend anti-expansion rallies was Bill Perkins, a state senator for Harlem. In a letter to the *New York Times*, Perkins expressed his opposition to the eminent domain laws and the process of public review: "New York's eminent domain laws are in need of reform. The Empire State Development Corporation's attempted taking of private property on behalf of Columbia University illustrates how the current process lacks accountability, transparency or meaningful public review."[29]

On December 18, 2008, the ESDC voted unanimously to invoke eminent domain against properties in the project footprint that were not owned by Columbia. On January 21, 2009, Tuck-it-Away Storage owner Nick Sprayregen and gas station owners Gurnam Singh and Parminder Kaur filed separate lawsuits in the New York Supreme Court, Appellate Division, challenging the ESDC's blight finding and approval of eminent domain.

In a surprise decision, the Appellate Division ruled 3–2 on December 3, 2009, that the state's use of eminent domain "to benefit an elite private institution" was in violation of the takings clause of the U.S. Constitution and article 1§7 of the New York State Constitution.[30] In the joint ruling on the Sprayregen and Singh-Kaur suits, the court also determined that the finding of blight was made in "bad faith," and that the ESDC's definition of blight was unconstitutionally vague. Justice Catterson wrote, "the blight designation in the instant case is mere sophistry. It was utilized by ESDC years after the scheme was hatched to justify the employment of eminent domain but this project has always primarily concerned a massive capital project for Columbia."[31]

However, on June 24, 2010, the New York State Court of Appeals, the state's highest court, overturned the Appellate Court finding by unanimous decision. Arguing that a private university can serve a "public purpose," Judge Carmen Ciparick wrote, "the indisputably public purpose of education is particularly vital for New York City and the State to maintain their respective statuses *as global centers of higher education and academic research*."[32] Ciparick's ruling echoed the language and line of argument Columbia had been using to justify the exercise of eminent domain and fulfill its "public purpose" requirement.

In early 2011, Columbia University began the demolition of structures in Manhattanville. From the fifteenth floor of the building where I lived (a Columbia faculty residence on the edge of the footprint), I watched buildings vanish, as if overnight, obliterating the spatial traces and relations of a two-hundred-year history.

No person or organization, to my knowledge, contested the university's right as a property owner to expand its campus into Manhattanville. As a faculty member, I was well aware of the university's chronic need for space. Rather, it was the university's insistence on exclusive control of the footprint—in the name of a subterranean "bathtub"—and the state's

28 PR 233–09, May 20, 2009.

29 *New York Times*, December 20, 2009.

30 *New York Times*, January 1, 2010.

31 *Wall Street Journal*, January 1, 2010.

32 *Columbia Spectator*, June 24, 2010; Emphasis added.

33 "Neighbors," http://neighbors.columbia.edu/pages/manplanning.

approval of eminent domain that incited outrage and protracted resistance among a broad spectrum of community-based interests. To that end, Columbia fashioned a narrative that constructed Manhattanville as a postindustrial "dead end," whose salvation could best be achieved through "smart growth"—growth that would resurrect Manhattanville "as a world center for knowledge, creativity, and solutions for society's challenges."[33]

The contrast between an obsolete present and a "smart future" provided the discursive framework for the blight finding and case for eminent domain. The AKRF neighborhood conditions study (and EarthTech's subsequent "audit") employed a rhetoric that emphasized the footprint's visual and physical isolation from surrounding area and the deteriorated state and "functional obsolescence" of existing structures. To overcome this opacity the university promised "transparency," an architectural ideal rooted in a modernist glass utopia and in anxieties concerning the disordered diversity of the street. This discourse of transparency and of a smart, cutting-edge future found its way into the documents of government agencies, the statements of politicians, and, perhaps most significantly, the decisions of the courts.

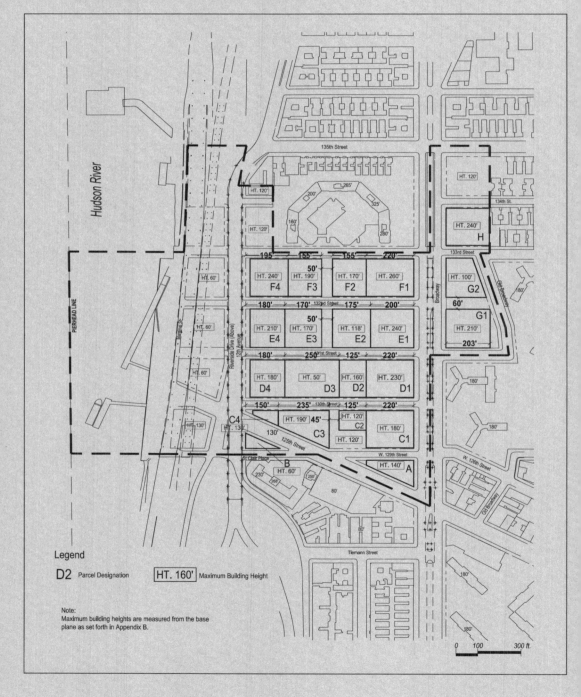

Hudson River

PIERHEAD LINE

135th Street

HT. 120'

HT. 120'

200'

265'

325'

160'

280'

HT. 120'

134th St.

HT. 240'

H

HT. 120'

HT. 60'

195'

155'

155'

220'

133rd Street

HT. 60'

HT. 240' | HT. 190' | HT. 170' | HT. 260'

50'

F4 | **F3** | **F2** | **F1**

HT. 100'

G2

180'

12th Avenue

Riverside Drive (Above)

132nd Street

180'

170'

175'

200'

60'

G1

HT. 60'

HT. 210' | HT. 170' | HT. 118' | HT. 240'

50'

E4 | **E3** | **E2** | **E1**

HT. 210'

203'

Broadway

Old Broadway

Marginal St.

180'

250'

125'

220'

131st Street

180'

HT. 60'

HT. 180' | HT. 50' | HT. 160' | HT. 230'

D4 | **D3** | **D2** | **D1**

150'

235'

125'

220'

130th Street

180'

HT. 130'

HT. 190' | 45' | HT. 120'

HT. 180'

C4 | **C3** | **C2** | **C1**

130'

125th Street

HT. 120'

HT. 120'

St. Clair Place

W. 129th Street

230'

250'

HT. 60' | **B**

HT. 140'

A

W. 126th Street

265'

80'

Old Broadway

180'

80'

Tiemann Street

180'

180'

Legend

D2 Parcel Designation | HT. 160' | Maximum Building Height

Note:
Maximum building heights are measured from the base
plane as set forth in Appendix B.

0   100   300 ft.

Parcel designation and building heights in the
Manhattanville Special Mixed-Use Academic
District, 2007. Courtesy of the New York City
Department of City Planning.

Special Manhattanville Mixed-Use District

In 2007, two years after the location search for Columbia University's campus expansion had begun, the New York City Department of City Planning approved the Special Manhattanville Mixed-Use District, zoned for "Academic Mixed-Use Development."[1] The first alteration to zoning in the area since the 1916 Zoning Resolution, the special district was created explicitly to accommodate the anticipated needs and uses of the new Columbia campus, the result of years of negotiation between university administration, the project's architects, and the city planning commission.

Dividing the seventeen-acre district into three use types—Academic Mixed-Use Area, Waterfront Area, and Mixed-Use Development Area—the resolution provided for community, residential, and recreational use and stipulated urban design regulations including ground-level transparency, open areas (called the Square, the Grove, the Small Square, and the East/West Open Area as written in the master plan), widened sidewalks, and street walls. By altering the building height limit and setback requirements, the resolution allowed for taller buildings, enabling the square footage needed for labs, classrooms, and galleries. It also emphasized flexibility in design, creating a condition that would adapt to the decades-long rollout of the campus. In des-

ignating the special district, the city also transferred what would have remained municipal property beneath street level to make possible the campus's below-grade service area.[2] Notably, manufacturing and light industrial uses, previously permitted, were not included in the updated district, and provisions for waterfront revitalization, apart from access to it, went undiscussed.

As an alternative to the proposed rezoning (which the university had drafted), West Harlem's Community Board 9 proposed its own plan for the district, calling for the preservation of existing housing and business (including some of the light industrial uses), the expansion of low-income housing, and community services on par with those students would be receiving. It also suggested creating a community benefits agreement, establishing a community land trust, and preventing any street de-mapping. The 197-a Plan (as community-formed plans are called) was developed with the Pratt Center and supported by the West Harlem Environmental Coalition, the Municipal Arts Society, the Harlem Tenants Council, residents of the NYCHA and Grant Houses, and the Housing Development Fund Corporation Council, but it was not approved by the City Planning Commission. Provisions of it were, however, incorporated into the special district zoning resolution,

including the establishment of tenant antiharassment programs, the condemnation of eminent domain programs, lower building heights, stipulation for more open space, and the inclusion of a wider range of retail and commercial functions. Significantly, by running the two proposals through the commission simultaneously, the review process stimulated conversation about what the Manhattanville design meant for neighborhood residents and what the desires of tenants, employees, and future students might be.

1
The City of New York Zoning Resolution, Article X: Special Purpose Districts, Chapter 4: Special Manhattanville Mixed Use District, most recently amended March 22, 2016.

2
Department of City Planning, City of New York, "197-A Plan for Community District 9," Spring 2008, 16, http://www.nyc.gov/html/mancb9/downloads/pdf/197_a_plan_brief.pdf.

By definition, universities establish and manage precincts, domains, "areas," and "fields." One way they do this is by drawing lines. In the American context, with its tradition of the college or university campus (from the Latin *campus*, or field), these lines begin with the boundary of the campus itself. Columbia University is no exception. In Morningside Heights the relevant lines are drawn most visibly in the brick, stone (or "cast" stone), iron, trees, and grass that demarcate the campus and sort its buildings into a departmental or disciplinary order redolent of the nineteenth century. In the new Manhattanville campus, avowedly interdisciplinary lines are drawn in steel and, most emphatically, in glass.

REINHOLD MARTIN

Columbia University's new Manhattanville campus was designed, essentially, by the New York–based architectural firm Skidmore, Owings & Merrill (SOM), in collaboration with a long list of technical experts, including the Renzo Piano Building Workshop (RPBW). For several generations, SOM has been the international archetype of a corporate architectural practice, in terms of both its clientele and its internal makeup. Currently, the firm—which is not technically incorporated but rather organized as a Limited Liability Partnership (LLP)—maintains ten offices in five different countries. Its self-identified expertise encompasses seven geographical regions (covering most of the world, except for Africa), in ten different market areas, and its professional services span eight different subfields, of which architecture is one.[1]

1 Skidmore, Owings & Merrill, "Expertise," http://www.som.com/expertise.

SOM has been designing corporate, collegiate, and university buildings and campuses almost since the firm's inception in the 1930s. Viewed dispassionately, the quality of their individual academic buildings, though varied, is not significantly different from the uneven efforts of architect-auteurs such as Renzo Piano. More often than not, Piano is given credit for the master plan of the Manhattanville campus and for the design of its current centerpiece, the Jerome L. Greene Science Center. But a closer look at the actual lines drawn suggests a more complex arrangement. Here, what matters most is not architectural authorship, whether designated by proper names or by acronyms, but the network of relations that draw and redraw the university itself.

Within this network, the architecture of Columbia's Manhattanville campus operates at two distinct but interconnected levels, that of representation and that of production. By representation I mean all of the virtualities—images, colors, names, forms—that circulate and congeal to produce a kind of order, or a recognizable domain of things, people, and processes that can itself be named: "Columbia," "Science," "Students," "Community." In Manhattanville, many of these arise *in silica*, both in glass and online. Silica operates here much like brick and stone do in Morningside Heights, as a marker of similarities and differences, a connector and a divider. Representation, then, is a material-based system of similarities and differences, connections and disconnections. By production I mean the cultural-technical manner in which that system is configured, how it is made, and how it makes what it makes—Columbia, science, students, community. That is, the network of material relations and processes through which, for example, a recognizably pallid shade of blue, in this case Benjamin Moore 1657 (or "Niagara Falls"), appears on the side of the Greene Science Center so that we of the Columbia "community" know it to be, in some vague sense, related to the university. Take that blue away—remove it from all the surfaces, graduation gowns, flags, sports uniforms, and logos—and the thing called Columbia ceases to be what it was before. The bond to which the paint alludes, formally consecrated as a bond between Pantone 290 (or Pantone 292, for sports) and "Columbia blue," binds representation and production into a single, indivisible complex.

Here is another example—the twin, white smokestacks that pierce the sky above the Greene Science Center, authored, technically, by RPBW, the building's design architects. In a lecture presented at Columbia's Graduate School of Architecture, Planning, and Preservation (GSAPP) in March 2016 and transcribed in this publication, RPBW's eponymous principal, Renzo Piano, referred to the laboratory building as a "factory." The twinned stacks, quite visibly adorned at night by a pair of blinking red lights, drill that image home. The image of the smokestack-factory therefore does the work of representation no more subtly than the quasi-Columbia blue that wraps the building's midriff. Nonetheless, it is uncannily anachronistic, in two ways. First, the building, home to Columbia's Mortimer B. Zuckerman Mind Brain Behavior Institute, is anything but a factory in the industrial sense. Second, it was exactly this anachronism that student protesters exploited in the 1960s with the epithet "knowledge factory" to describe the postindustrial alliance of university research, big business, and the military.

Piano, whose career is an epic tale of genuine personal grace and artistry deployed in the service of what today's student protesters might call soft neoliberalism (despite his evident best intentions), thus speaks a kind of inadvertent historical truth with his deadpan architectural metaphor. Technically, the boiler stacks atop the Greene Science Center simply vent the products of combustion from the campus's central heating plant. But they also prominently announce another function. They ask us to ask: What will this factory produce? No doubt, researchers at the Mind Brain Behavior Institute will produce groundbreaking and possibly lifesaving scientific knowledge; and yes, some of that knowledge will also have commercial and even military value, directly or indirectly, in the sense addressed by the 1960s protesters. However, in the near future, most of this value (with the exception of patents) will likely be realized in spinoffs from university-based primary research rather than from the work done in the academic laboratories directly. As the strained factory metaphor demonstrates, the commodity more reliably made in the Greene Science Center and in the Manhattanville campus is, simply, meaning.

The question that follows is therefore not "What does the new campus mean?" but rather "How does the new campus make meaning, and what, in turn, does that meaning make?" The university website declares that "there are no gates on the new Manhattanville campus."[2] Yet an enigmatic pair of twinned, boxy, building-size vents along the future tree-lined promenade immediately to the west of the new Lenfest Center for the Arts suggests otherwise. The vents, which are temporary, provide ventilation and exhaust for the central energy plant directly below. Like the smokestacks, their placement, pairing, and design distinguish them from merely utilitarian structures and draw them into the order of representation. They form a kind of abandoned gate, severed from its usual boundary and unsure of which direction to face. Other architects of Piano's generation, and perhaps those who work for them, may remember many other such figures set adrift in a sea of uncertainty—including the vents popping up into the plaza of the Centre Pompidou in Paris, which Piano also designed with Richard Rogers. But the sources, whether conscious or unconscious, do not matter. It is as if the campus gate must be reproduced and even commemorated, precisely because it has been abolished.

Next to this temporary, sideways memorial to obsolete gates, the smaller arts building seems eager to reproduce the massing of Marcel Breuer's old, elegant Whitney Museum—now abandoned by its original owner in favor of a Piano-designed, ship-like Whitney-on-the-Hudson. Put the new Whitney and the Greene Science Center together and you get a pair of stranded modernist figures: an uptown factory and a downtown ocean liner. Like the Centre Pompidou, the twinned smokestacks and twinned vents uptown reverse the standard order—building-as-machine becomes machine-as-building. The difference being that in New York most of the machine is underground. In his lecture, describing the permeability of the Manhattanville master plan with its through-streets and its city blocks, Piano referred to a planned seven-story below-grade structure spanning the entire site that, in his words, "holds it all together."[3] Regardless of the ultimate extent of the underground megabuilding, which currently extends four stories below grade and is limited to the perimeter of Phase One, the unity implied is

2   Columbia University, "Campus Plan," http://www.manhattanville.columbia.edu/campus-plan.

3   Renzo Piano, lecture at Columbia University Graduate School of Architecture, Planning, and Preservation, New York, March 11, 2015, https://www.youtube.com/watch?v=4skqxww05U8.

Mechanical, Electrical, Plumbing BIM model
rendering of the Jerome L. Greene Science
Center. Courtesy of Jacobs Consultants.

131

more than technological. For, like the simultaneously rebuilt World Trade Center in Lower Manhattan—a project also led backstage by SOM on a site of comparable size and complexity using a similar underground "bathtub"—Columbia's new Manhattanville campus is, in principle, both several buildings and a single building, at once.

Most of what lies below grade and connects the academic buildings planned for Phase One is infrastructure: heating and cooling, parking, and building services. Like the smokestacks and vents, this infrastructure periodically reveals itself above ground in the form of elevator cores, ductwork, and electrical conduits to organize the urban field. A color-coded digital model of the Greene Science Center shows the subterranean links that connect the smokestacks and the rest of the building's mechanical systems to the central energy plant. A related, probably earlier, diagram of the planned underground building in Piano's hand shows the plant flanked by vivaria, parking, and loading docks, with an "Olympic swimming pool" adjacent to the existing Studebaker Building. As built, the field is punctuated above and below by a structural column grid, which outlines the site's present and future "buildings." All of which are, or will be, simply aboveground extensions of the underground building, with their volumes determined principally by the calibration of shell to core measured out by the columns.

A basement is like a building's unconscious, containing all kinds of secrets. In this case, the open secret is not the wished-for swimming pool awaiting a willing donor; it is the very existence of the massive underground building itself. In an interview with Caitlin Blanchfield, also included in this volume, SOM partner and GSAPP alumnus Anthony Vacchione acknowledges the plan's debts:

> In the Morningside campus of nearly a hundred years ago, McKim, Mead & White ingeniously put together a large, below-grade system of corridors, with Low Library extending out to Avery Hall and Uris Hall. That was a huge invention, that everything can be serviced from below to create this significant, monumental building complex. Could we do the same in Manhattanville, at the neighborhood scale? We had worked extensively with Disney, and with Disney everything disappears. It's magic. So that was the other thing that we started exploring: how to tie all this below-grade so you could service everything, and then also to accommodate all the parking that we knew was going to be a requirement of the site.[4]

From McKim, Mead & White to Disney: The comparison is telling. It not only distinguishes an imagistic (representational, metaphor-ridden) upstairs from an infrastructural (technical, nonsignifying) downstairs, but also it explains the relation between the project's urbanism and its architecture. The university campus becomes a collection of symbolic buildings popping out of a comparatively undifferentiated, invisible, machine-like base, like at Disneyland but also like the south campus at Morningside Heights.

In the same interview, SOM partner Marilyn Taylor, speaking politically about the streets that pass through the site, describes the "great urban grid of New York City" as "democratic and inclusive."[5] Hence, like the underground building that they interrupt, the through-streets are more than practical; they, too, signify. But how? The New York street grid is also an efficient means for dividing up urban space into units of property that can be bought and sold as real estate. Only those urban elements such as parks, streets, schools, hospitals, prisons, and so on that are designated as "public" are to some limited degree exempt from the rule of profit that ultimately prevails in real estate markets. Also partially protected are public housing complexes, such as the Manhattanville Houses directly across Broadway and the Grant Houses nearby. Throughout the city's five boroughs, many of these housing complexes interrupt the street grid, with large amounts of unbuilt land surrounding them. Increasingly, politicians, policy makers, and developers have viewed this land as real estate, the potential value of which increases with the gentrification of the surrounding neighborhood.

At the level of representation, which operates quite pragmatically, the streets passing through the campus substitute one public for another. Referring to concerns among Harlem residents that the new campus would accelerate gentrification, especially in the area of housing, Taylor notes that as the project was being designed, "Maintaining public housing together with building new affordable and market-rate units was already becoming a big challenge for New York."[6] She does not acknowledge the solution proposed by the Bloomberg administration while Manhattanville was being planned, a solution not entirely taken off the table by the De Blasio administration: the quasi-privatization of public housing through the sale or leasing of open land on public housing sites to real estate developers. Since both the Manhattanville Houses and the Grant Houses are potential targets for such a policy, the resistance of residents is not surprising. Taylor's language is precise: public housing is to be "maintained," while only "affordable" and "market-rate" housing is to be built. In other words, no more public housing even on publicly owned land. This is an accurate restatement of governing practices that have systematically defunded public services in favor of market-led "solutions," beginning with housing. Thus, as public streets are celebrated, public housing is bracketed.

The land around that housing is the historical consequence of the multi-block "tower-in-the park" planning approach characteristic of 1950s and 1960s urban renewal programs, which authorized the "demapping" of certain streets (erasing parts of the city grid, along with their neighborhoods) in order to build large-scale housing complexes on a single, unified site. Also in the 1960s, a similar planning approach yielded the original World Trade Center. Describing the new Columbia campus, Taylor exclaims: "no superblocks!" She is

4 Anthony Vacchione in "Master Planners as New Yorkers: An Interview with Marilyn Taylor, Anthony Vacchione, Lois Mazzitelli, and Philip Palmgren," in this volume, 36.

5 See Marilyn Taylor in "New Yorkers," 40.

6 See Marilyn Taylor in "New Yorkers," 41.

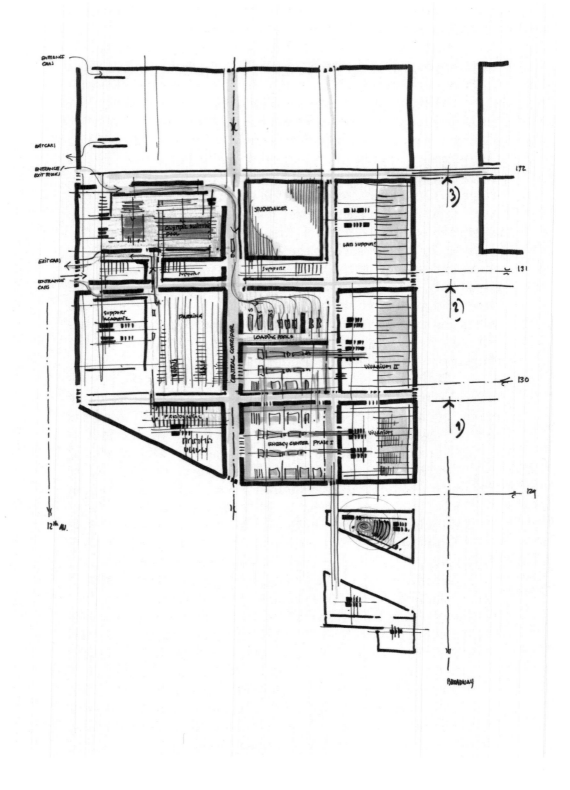

**Sketch of the underground plan for the
Jerome L. Greene Science Center.
Courtesy of Renzo Piano Building Workshop.**

clearly referring to the widespread backlash against such planning since that time, which also guided the rebuilding of downtown. But the real destructiveness of urban renewal and the consequent ghettoization of populations have also frequently been used to stigmatize, and hence to delegitimize, large-scale state intervention in the housing markets, especially when that intervention favors the underclass. Intended or not, this is another, historically precise meaning of "no superblocks!"

And yet, like the rebuilt World Trade Center, Columbia's new campus is nothing if not a superblock, underground. That is, it is a superblock that goes to great lengths to open itself up. It allows streets to pass through it, just as the glass wrapping the Greene Science Center makes quotidian knowledge-making visible from those streets and the subway platform above it. As Taylor suggests, the resulting zone will be more physically accessible at street level than the Morningside campus. But this seeming inversion, of open-and-transparent versus solid-and-enclosed, conceals a deeper affinity. For times have changed since 1897, when the Morningside campus first opened. Transparency, which at that time was already becoming the avatar of an open future, is no longer that. Both at the level of representation and the level of its material effects, glass does not equal democracy. Everyone knows that there are ways of drawing lines and marking limits other than fortifying them in brick and stone. Renzo Piano himself said as much in his lecture at Columbia: "Transparency is safer [i.e., more secure] than opacity."[7] The authority to make these claims comes from many years of making glass buildings and securing glass cities—as in the Piano-led Potsdamer Platz commercial redevelopment astride the former wall zone in Berlin. Long after, the expression "the wall in the head" described the persistence of lines that all the glass in the world cannot erase, including the glass dome that Piano's peer, Norman Foster, installed over the Reichstag in a singularly heavy-handed effort to replace one symbolic regime with another.

7 Piano, lecture, 2015.

The question, then, is what the real effects of the transparent effort to produce transparency in Manhattanville will be. Time will tell. For now, there remains the paradox of the twinned smokestacks atop the scientific knowledge factory and the twinned vents below. Figures of industry astride a recently demolished industrial zone, they are traces of the great underground machine that will help the university do what it must do. By its very nature, however, that machine must visibly disappear. What is more, its visible invisibility must be made to mean something—openness, publicness, "democracy"—even as the campus requires a line around it that cannot and should not be erased, grids and glass notwithstanding.

For the university is not the polis. It is, rather, a distorted mirror image of the polis that must maintain a certain distance—a distance that the Western critical tradition has called autonomy—in order to do its work. Thus the earlier Morningside campus originally sat, Acropolis-like, upon a crest at the northern edge of Manhattan in a manner that was both aloof from the great urban engine and deeply integrated into its business cycles, as the names engraved on its buildings attest. Today, the new campus reverses the equation, gesturing toward the surrounding city rather than withdrawing from it. In doing so, however, it does not reflect the inherent conflicts and contradictions that divide the urban field. Instead, as an inverted image of the "original" Morningside campus, it reflects mostly itself.

To put this self-citation in perspective, it is worth remembering that Columbia has at least one other campus, farther uptown: the Columbia University Medical Center. Some of the most academically prominent inhabitants of the Greene Science Center will, in fact, migrate downtown from laboratories currently located on that campus. Even as it works so hard to build an inverse mirror image of Morningside Heights, the Manhattanville campus turns its back on Washington Heights and the medical center there. This may be because it is difficult to discern anything like a classical "campus" uptown. It may also be because the intimate sociotechnical relationship of the hospital with the communities around it cannot be easily replicated. Still, the heterogeneous, slightly chaotic ensemble of buildings around the hospital is far more recognizably urban than anything that SOM or RPBW have conjured farther south. Like the Pantone blue, take that campus away and you no longer have "Columbia." So why not tilt the mirror slightly uptown, and reflect (upon) an urbanity quite different from the one that opposes transparency to opacity, or glass-and-steel to brick-and-stone?

SOM's Philip Palmgren answers this question preemptively when describing Manhattanville's underground structure: "It's actually creating a symbiotic relationship between all the buildings and making them all function as a single sort of entity."[8] The desired unity is simultaneously technical and symbolic. In this case, however, the two levels are both synchronized and at odds—doubled up into an invisible, integrated machine below and a coordinated field of discrete units above. Between them is a proliferation of gates: doors, card swipes, service stairs, access panels, elevators, plumbing, laboratory fixtures, and so on. But the campus gate always faces in two directions at once. Seen from the inside, its heraldry and its infrastructures reproduce the self-image and the material reality of a body set apart from the polis, admission to which is strictly regulated, where unusual freedoms bring unusual responsibilities. Seen from the outside, however, it's just a gate, another opening like the gap between two smokestacks or two vents, passage through which signifies nothing. Tasked with making meaning, Manhattanville's planners seem to have assumed that it is inherently meaningful to walk through a campus and to see into its buildings. From this perspective, the apparent absence of gates is just as meaningful. But this is the view from the inside, which, trained by the Disney Imagineers, peers through mirrors made of transparent glass and sees an enchanted forest. If anything like meaning is to be produced inside or outside the knowledge factory, it will more likely be found in the thickness of the fragile, ambivalent line at the campus edge, wherever that edge may be.

8 Philip Palmgren in "Master Planners as New Yorkers," 39.

Biographies

Amale Andraos is Dean of Columbia University's Graduate School of Architecture, Planning, and Preservation and co-founder of WORKac, a New York-based architectural and urban practice with international reach. In addition to Columbia, Andraos has taught at universities including Princeton University School of Architecture, Harvard Graduate School of Design, University of Pennsylvania Design School, and the American University of Beirut. Her publications include *The Arab City: Architecture and Representation*; *49 Cities*; *Above the Pavement, the Farm!*; and numerous essays. WORKac is focused on reimaging architecture at the intersection of the urban, the rural, and the natural. It has achieved international recognition through institutional projects such as the Edible Schoolyards; a new conference center in Libreville, Gabon; or the Miami Collage Garage. In addition to other awards, WORKac was named the 2015 AIA New York State Firm of the Year.

Carol Becker is Professor of the Arts and Dean of Columbia University School of the Arts. Before coming to Columbia University she was Dean of Faculty at The School of the Art Institute of Chicago. She is the author of several books including *Thinking in Place: Art, Action, and Cultural Production; The Invisible Drama: Women and the Anxiety of Change; Surpassing the Spectacle: Global Transformations and the Changing Politics of Art; The Subversive Imagination: Artists and Social Responsibility* and the forthcoming *Losing Helen*. She writes regularly for print and online publications.

Caitlin Blanchfield is a PhD candidate at Columbia University's Graduate School of Architecture, Planning, and Preservation, and a contributing editor to the *Avery Review*.

Diller Scofidio + Renfro (DS+R) integrates architecture, the visual arts, and the performing arts. Founding partners Diller and Scofidio are recipients of the MacArthur Foundation "Genius" award. DS+R's architectural work includes The High Line and Lincoln Center for the Performing Arts renovation and expansion in New York City, The Broad in Los Angeles, and the Institute of Contemporary Arts in Boston. The studio's independent works have been exhibited at leading cultural institutions around the globe, including the San Francisco Museum of Modern Art, Palais De Tokyo in Paris, the Metropolitan Museum of Art, and the Whitney Museum in New York.

Elizabeth Diller, a founding partner at DS+R, is a Professor of Architecture at Princeton University's School of Architecture. She attended Cooper Union School of Art and received a Bachelor of Architecture from Cooper Union School of Architecture.

Charles Renfro is a partner at DS+R—a position he has held since 2004, after joining the firm in 1997. Renfro has taught at Rice University, Parsons School of Design, School of Visual Arts, and the Graduate School of Architecture, Planning, and Preservation at Columbia University. He attended Rice University and received a Master of Architecture degree from Columbia University.

Dr. Steven Gregory is a Professor of Anthropology and African-American Studies at Columbia University. His research focuses on the intersection of race, class, and gender in the formation of political subjectivities, social hierarchies, and urban-based social movements. Gregory is the author of *The Devil Behind the Mirror: Globalization and Politics in the Dominican Republic* (University of California Press, 2007), *Santería in New York City: A Study in Cultural Resistance* (Garland, 2007), and *Black Corona: Race and the Politics of Place in an Urban Community* (Princeton University Press, 1998); as well as the co-editor of *Race* (Rutgers University Press, 1994). Gregory is currently working on a historical study of the "American Acropolis," the constellation of elite cultural and educational institutions in Northern Manhattan.

Maxine Griffith holds the title of Executive Vice President for Government and Community Affairs at Columbia University and Special Advisor for Campus Planning. Griffith brings a strong background in urban planning and design to her role as a key member of the leadership team planning for the university's 17 acre, six billion dollar Manhattan-ville campus. From 2000 to 2005, she served as Executive Director of the Philadelphia City Planning Commission and Secretary (Deputy Mayor) for Strategic Planning. Prior to this, Griffith served in the Clinton administration at the U.S. Department of Housing and Urban Development (HUD), first as the Regional Director for New York and New Jersey, and then in Washington as HUD's Assistant Deputy Secretary. She was an appointee to the New York City Planning Commission, a post that she held for six years. Born in Harlem, Griffith holds a Master of Architecture degree from the University of California, Berkeley. She has taught city planning and urban design at Columbia University, New York University, and the University of Pennsylvania.

Thomas M. Jessell is the Claire Tow Professor in the Departments of Neuroscience and Biochemistry and Molecular Biophysics at